Raindrops

How Meditation Changed the Course of My Life

Shirish Patel, M.D.

Cover design: Team Miblart
Editing and interior design: Rachel L. Hall, Writely Divided

ISBN: 978-05788-179-6-5 Paperback edition
ISBN: 978-05788-179-7-2 eBook edition

Raindrops: How Meditation Changed the Course of My Life / Shirish Patel, M.D. —1st ed.

To my daughter, Suhina

May your path be illuminated with spiritual wisdom

as mine was by Ba, my spiritual teacher,

& by Sri Eknath Easwaran, my spiritual guru.

Contents

Contents

Contents

Raindrops

Part I
PLACES AND TIMES

One:

Early Life in Uganda

1955–1972

I resolve to be mindful of the motive behind my work. I will examine my motives to make sure that they are in harmony with my spiritual ideal.

—from Swami Tyagananda's
Walking the Walk: A Karma Yoga Manual

The ping-pong paddle

I was about nine years old playing cricket with my friends in the small yard next to our house which we fondly referred to as The Ground. Suddenly, a ping-pong paddle landed next to me. I picked it up and recognized it as mine. An edge had cracked and there was mud stuck on one side. I became furious. My most prized sports possession was ruined.

I turned around and saw my youngest brother, Mayoor, standing behind me on a slight elevation about twenty feet away. *There was the culprit.*

Cursing, I threw the paddle at him.

Over fifty-five years have elapsed since that day, but my memories of it remain as vivid as if it were yesterday.

The paddle struck Mayoor in the back of his head, and he started bleeding profusely. Our house servant, Petro, was standing nearby. He ran towards my brother, shouting at me in Swahili, "*Wewe Shirishi!* What have you done?"

There was a lot of commotion. My parents emerged from the house, followed by a family friend who was visiting. Fortunately, the visitor was a doctor. He ran to his car to retrieve his medical kit while Petro stemmed the bleeding with a rag. The doctor patched up Mayoor and reassured my parents he would be fine.

By this time, I had run back to my bedroom. I cowered in a corner, waiting for the inevitable. My older sister Shobhi came in and berated me.

"You are in deep trouble, *Shirishi*," Shobhi scolded, calling me by Petro's Swahili version of my name.

I felt petrified. I prayed for our guest to stay longer. Maybe he would even stay the night since he was visiting from out of town. That would save my skin.

At least some of it.

A car engine started. No luck: our visitor wasn't staying. A few moments later, footsteps ominously stomped outside my bedroom door.

I backed up on my bed, trying to get even further into the wall, and covered my face, expecting the worst. But the blows that rained down on me were soft. Was my father, with his large ex-farmer's hands, going easy on me? No. It was my mother. Her bare hands coupled with her slim, petite build could muster only so much force. Fortunately for me, she had beaten my father to the punishment cell.

And even more fortunately, she had not brought her rolling pin.

I remember little about the days that followed, except that I frequently checked on Mayoor. Mostly, I kept to myself and made an extra effort to keep my tongue in check when my older siblings chastised me. My father counseled me—for the hundredth time—against throwing things in anger. And my mother's tears of frustration and shame only compounded my remorse.

My struggles with anger would continue well into middle age until I came across the writings of a gentleman who would become my spiritual guru.

The year 1955

Mbale is a charming city in southeastern Uganda near the border with its neighbor, Kenya. On a cloudless day, one can see Mount Elgon, a volcanic mountain with one of the largest calderas in the world. For me, the view of its spur, the Nkokonjeru Range, benevolently standing sentinel to the east of the city, is how I remember my birthplace. With naked eyes, one could see the waterfalls cascading down its face. With minor effort, one could make out villagers carrying loads of *matoke* (a type of banana) or firewood delicately balanced on their heads as they traversed the trails, crisscrossing its gentle slopes.

The year of my birth, 1955, was a blessed year for the world. It was the year in which one of the greatest discoveries in medicine was made: the polio vaccine.

But for my family, the vaccine would come a day too late.

Of our family's six children, my sister Shobhana, lovingly called by all as Shobhi, is the eldest sibling. She is followed by Arun, me, Narendra, nicknamed Nanu, Mayoor, and Meeta.

My father, Vaghjibhai, whom we siblings addressed as *bapuji*, was a civil servant. My mother, Kantaben, whom we called *ba*, made sure we were well-clothed, fed, and quiet, especially when my father was sleeping.

The oldest five were each born two years apart, thanks to breast-feeding acting as a natural birth control tool. My youngest sister was born ten years after my youngest brother, so she was fourteen years younger than me. I felt deeply ashamed when I learnt about her impending arrival. To an adolescent, pregnancy meant sex. And *sex* was a dirty word.

I vowed never to have any children of my own.

My mother: My spiritual teacher

My mother has always been a dainty woman. Yet her elfin features belie her remarkable inner strength.

Born into a farming family in a small village called Atkot, my mother was the second oldest of eight children, but her exact age is somewhat in question. Two generations would pass before the modern practice of issuing birth certificates reached her village. Atkot is located in an arid, drought-stricken region of the northwest state of Gujarat in India. After consulting with the living village "almanac" (relatives, elders, and priests) and considering various mathematical permutations such as my eldest sibling's age, I figure she was born around 1932. Her birth name was Rambhaben. But after she was married, her in-laws changed her name to one they considered more modern, Kantaben.

When she was growing up, her family could not afford to adorn her with jewelry. They settled for the next best solution—a permanent solution. Tattoos. In later life, the small, round ink dots on her knuckles and forearms would cause endless fascination amongst many who met her beyond the shores of India.

In her younger years, my mother would tie her hair with colorful ribbons in a plait so long it brushed the floor. Women from her era, and especially from her background, did not flaunt their beauty, nor did they discuss vanities. But I often heard ladies complimenting my mother's beauty behind her back, particularly when she wore bright, colorful saris at weddings and on other special occasions.

Her family's sole source of income was the small farm her father owned near their village. The land had more stones and boulders than tillable soil. It is small wonder, then, that my mother's memories of her childhood are filled with impressions of working long hours in scorching heat. Her tiny hands picked up and carried pebbles from the field and dumped them into an oxcart all day long until her work time was relieved by the setting sun. Then she relished her meager meal of *chapattis* and chilies. Often, it would be her only meal of the day.

Despite the back-breaking labor they did, the family was not able to make ends meet. In a desperate act of survival, my grandfather was forced to give two of my uncles into bonded labor. On the landlord's farm, each of my uncles was yoked to an ox. So paired, the beasts of burden—one man, one animal—tilled farmland for seven grueling months.

With her family so deep in grinding poverty, it is not surprising that neither my mother nor any of her siblings ever set foot in a school.

My mother was only thirteen years old when she married my father, who was twelve years older. Soon after their marriage, she left India to join my father in Mbale, Uganda. As a child-bride, a million miles from her family, and in a totally alien environment, her new life must have been bewildering and scary.

1.1 – My mother and father, c. 1949

Fortunately, her neighbor, Dahimasi, took my mother under her wings.

Dahimasi was about fifteen years older than my mother. She had three sons, the eldest of whom, Kanubhai, would come to live with us in Kampala for the better part of my childhood. If there is a kinder-hearted woman somewhere, I have not met her. Tall and elegant, Dahimasi worked at the speed of a roadrunner, advocated voraciously for underdogs, and always placed others' welfare before her own. Even after returning to India following her husband's retirement, she sent us gifts of clothing for many years. Whenever we four brothers stepped out in matching shirts, Dahimasi's munificence was on full display.

Dahimasi trained my mother in household matters and social obligations. Within a short time, she helped my mother mature from child-bride to devoted wife and later into a nurturing mother. Dahimasi would become godmother to all my siblings and me.

My father, ever the educator, tried to teach my mother English. She went as far as learning to write her name. After that, progress was halted forever. Our family has our guesses for the short-lived tutorials from my father. My father's camp thinks our mother simply couldn't be bothered or was just too stubborn. My mother's camp (which includes me) believes our father's lack of patience and fiery temper could not have helped matters.

To her credit, my mother taught herself to read in Gujarati, her mother tongue. As far back as I can remember, she has always been a voracious reader. I can picture her sitting on the floor, deeply engrossed in reading an abridged version of the *Mahabharata* cradled in a plinth, much like a priest in a temple poring over his scriptural studies. This ancient Indian epic is more than a thousand pages long. I don't believe she would have been daunted at all if she had to read the original version, which is ten times the length of the *Iliad* and *Odyssey* combined. My mother's well of patience has always been deep—in contrast to my father's.

For someone without any formal education, my mother's knowledge of the Hindu scriptures is remarkably broad and deep. Her knowledge has been fortified by her habit of listening to discourses given by prominent Indian sages. Her favorites were Shankaracharya Maharaj, Rang Avadhoot, and Morari Bapu. As a child, I sat with her for hours as she wove many of the stories and lives of seemingly unrelated hundreds of Indian deities into cohesive and entertaining parables.

I regret not having such conversations with her more often.

As a teenager, I had a tendency to readily pass judgment on others, especially relatives and family friends.

I was easily awed by people's material possessions. Within a fraction of a second, I would form an opinion about a person by comparing his or her possessions with ours. If neighbors bought a new car, I deemed them richer than us, and therefore, I assumed they were arrogant. If an auntie wore sparkling jewelry, she was better off than my mother and a show-off. If a family friend purchased a tape recorder to play Bollywood songs, they were modern, and we were not sophisticated. My family possessed a car, but most of my friends' families did not: therefore, they were not in the same league as we were. I extended such comparisons to academic accomplishments as well. If I scored better grades in class, I was erudite, and the rest were not so clever.

These kinds of ruminations were my constant companions—sometimes, I entertained them consciously, but often, subconsciously. It was as if I was carrying some sort of mental tool to benchmark others' social status or intelligence. My mother would patiently listen to my pronouncements. Then she would offer a counterpoint, usually in the form of a parable.

One day, she related an incident about Rama, the legendary prince whose life is narrated in the Hindu epic, *Ramayana*.

> Rama and his friends were out hunting when they came to a small river. The fishermen on the shores fell head over heels to try to earn the privilege of ferrying their beloved prince across the river.
>
> Back in the royal court, some of the fishermen complained to the prince. The fisherman he had selected to ferry him across the river, they said, was going about the village bragging he was the chosen one amongst them because the prince had picked his boat over the others. The fishermen were deeply despondent at having lost the opportunity to serve their master.

Rama responded that the feelings of the fishermen on both sides were misplaced. Superiority and inferiority complexes were both illnesses of the mind. Both emotions were negative and harmful in the long run.

It would take me a long time before I would be able to shed either of them.

Sometimes my mother would try and engage me in debates to test whether I could come up with an answer to my own dilemma. When the discussion came to a point where I knew I was losing, I would end it abruptly with a flippant remark: "If only you knew better!"

Unlike my father, my mother would never belittle me by describing my behavior as sophomoric or call me immature. Instead, she would simply recite one of her favorite sayings:

"Peepal paan kharntaa, hasti kupadiya. Muj veeti tuj veetase, dheeri baapudiya."

"As the mature leaves from the Peepal tree fall, the buds laugh. Says the mature leaf, 'What is happening to me will happen to you too. Just wait and see my dear.'"

An adage for life.

Even beyond my teen years, I had a tendency to blurt out the first words that came to my mind. More often than not, my response was emotionally driven. I saw no point in chewing my words when I *knew* I was right. It never occurred to me that my brash assessments or my verbal diarrhea could hurt other's feelings.

In her own gentle way, my mother would counsel me: "*Nah bolva ma naav guna,*" which means, "Silence has nine attributes."

I would counter with a wise-ass retort: "*Bole tena bor vechay,*" which translates, "He who speaks, sells the berries."

She would shake her head in resignation.

My mother was a master of idioms, adages, and proverbs. My tendency to use idiomatic language in everyday conversation probably comes from her.

I remember my mother intensely studying the scriptures when I was about twelve years old. She devoted her time to them, day and night, for several weeks at a stretch. She would take short breaks to dictate letters to me to send to her mentor and closest friend, Dahimasi, in India. Afterwards, she would return to her preoccupation. Most of the housework was left to Shobhi, my older sister.

She would start off dictating calmly: inquiring after Dahimasi's health, hoping that she was adjusting well in her new environment, and wishing God would continue to look over her and protect her and family.

Then, tears would start flowing.

Perhaps she missed her best friend. Or maybe she missed her own family. Or something she'd read in the scriptures might have provoked her emotions. Or the constant fights with my father over money had taken their toll. While we always had food on the table and our other basic needs were adequately met, there was little money for treats or pastimes. My mother scrimped and saved what she could from the grocery money so we could buy chewing gum or go to a soccer game. Her frugality made it possible for us to indulge.

I never discovered the reasons underlying her sadness. I recall yelling and shouting at her: *Stop weeping!* I could not handle her overt expressions of grief. Perhaps at a subconscious level, I did not want to see a person whom I considered omnipotent break down. She would pause for long moments, staring straight ahead, seemingly lost in thought. Suddenly, she would snap out of it and continue with her dictation. She bore her pain and suffering in silence.

I suspect now she must have been clinically depressed. Years later, my psychiatric training would lend credence to my impression. The letter writing was her attempt at catharsis.

One day as I played with friends on The Ground, I saw a recently widowed family friend give something to my mother. After the woman left, I asked what it was. My mother explained she had lent her friend twenty Uganda shillings a few months earlier, and she had come to repay the money.

In the early 1970s, twenty shillings, about two and one-half dollars, was no small change. I must have looked shocked. My mother explained that after the woman's husband passed away, she and her daughter were going through a rough patch. My mother had loaned the money to tide her over through the crisis. "Every family has needs," she explained, "and some people's needs are greater than ours."

I paused and reflected on her selflessness and generosity. My mother was loaning money when the primary cause of disagreements between her and my father was money itself.

A family friend stopped by one evening. This gentleman had at one time occupied a prestigious and well-salaried position. But he had lost everything to drink and had fallen on hard times. He was returning to India and had stopped over to visit before leaving Uganda.

He and my father were chatting in the living room. My mother was busy in the kitchen. I hovered nearby, anxious to know if his son, who was a very good friend of mine, was leaving the country with him. They lived in another town, so I had not seen my friend in a while.

Midway through their conversation, my father invited the gentleman to join us for dinner, but he declined. A few minutes later, my father got up and went to the kitchen. Our family ate all meals together, so I followed him. My mother immediately pulled me aside and asked me to go back and keep the visitor company. After serving my father, she came out of the kitchen and invited the visitor to join us for dinner. He again politely declined, muttered some excuse, and left.

The following morning, my mother explained why she had made me go back to our visitor. "Bestowing good fortune and taking it away is God's work. Money is like dirt on your hands. One wash, and it's all gone," she said. She told me I should never respect nor disrespect a person for what he or she has. She encouraged me to see the human being beneath it all.

She also had a few choice words for my father's behavior.

My mother has always maintained a remarkable ability to move on in life. She has been able to develop strong and caring bonds with the children of people who had once humiliated and abashed her.

One such family was that of my father's distant cousin who had helped him move to Uganda. The cousin's wife preferred to associate only with the fat cats of society. It was not surprising that she had little time for my penniless mother who had just arrived from India. She considered my mother a country bumpkin and was ashamed of her village-style couture of *chaniya choli* and *odhni*. Moreover, my mother spoke in her village dialect, further accentuating her rural upbringing. So whenever Madame Elite had visitors, she banished my mother to a side room.

But time is a great leveler.

A few years after my father's cousin and his family returned to India, his oldest daughter passed away. She and her two boys had stayed back in Kampala where her husband ran a thriving business. Soon after her death, as it was important to maintain family ties, her youngest sister's marriage was arranged with her brother-in-law. The bereaved husband, his two sons, and the newly married couple would all live under one roof. The two pre-teen boys needed a mother figure in the house.

Decades later, the sister shared with me how difficult she had found meeting the demands of her new role as a wife and as a caregiver for her two nephews. She was coping with her own sister's death, and she had no mother at hand to lend her moral support. "But," she told me, "your mother stepped in. After that, there was not a single day that I felt my own mother was not with me."

My mother took the new bride under her wings, just as she had been taken in decades earlier by Dahimasi.

I always considered my mother to be complaisant. Yet, one family issue gnawed at her.

In our family as I was growing up, money was always a contentious issue. There was barely enough. Having to dip into the cookie jar to meet the unrelenting demands of my father's relatives in India further depleted the coffer.

A typical scenario would unfold like this. At dinnertime, my father would announce a letter had come from India. Mail was collected from a post office box because home delivery service in Uganda did not exist. After dinner, we would all sit down on the floor, and my father would take an armchair. With great relish, he would ceremoniously slit open the blue aerogramme letter. He would read it aloud while the rest of us listened with feigned interest. There would be the usual mention of how poorly the farm was doing. The monsoons had failed, the plow-ox had died, or the birds had eaten the sown seeds. We knew what was coming. My father's voice softened noticeably as he read aloud the amount requested. And as always, there was that not-so-subtle threat that if my father could not remit the requested funds, there would be no option but to mortgage the farmland.

Reading the word *mortgage* must have felt like a dagger in his heart. My father had left his country, toiled at multiple jobs, remitted money back home, and sacrificed in a myriad of other ways so that he could free up his family's mortgaged land. And he'd done it all single-handedly. Now, these same folks he'd selflessly given to were hanging a sword over his head!

"Well, there goes my new pair of sneakers," I would mutter aloud.

The family would not be getting a tape recorder that year, either. If my older siblings felt personally deprived, they did not voice it publicly.

My mother could not understand why my father would not stand up to his family's relentless demands. She felt short-changed. And justifiably so. The remittances to India left little of my father's low salary for her children.

At times, my father would rub salt into the wound. He would declare that spending money on fancy clothes or shoes or a tape recorder or going to the movies were profligate habits.

The blue aerogrammes kept coming. Different dates. Same message. Like a bad penny, they showed up again and again.

My mother continued to fume inwardly. I have often wondered if there were another reason for my mother's antipathy towards some of her in-laws—a more personal one.

My maternal grandfather had arranged for my mother and her younger sister to marry my father and his nephew, respectively, on the same day. Double weddings between two families are a common practice in India even today. Often, a brother and his sister from one family will wed siblings from another family on the same day. It is simply economical.

For most Indian families, a daughter's wedding is their single most expensive undertaking. Fathers start saving for their daughter's wedding from the day they are born. Mothers amass saris, gold, and jewelry until the nuptial night. It is not at all unusual for families to slide into heavy debt as they put up a few days' show for their kith and kin. After all, they've got to outdo the Patels next door!

Unfortunately, my aunt's marriage did not last long. Her husband's sister-in-law had her eyes on him for her own sister. It is not difficult to imagine how unbearable my aunt's life would have been living in a hovel bursting at its seams with offspring from three generations, at the mercy of a martinet and her henpecked husband.

After I retired a few years ago, I started spending winters in India. My mother would join me from London, where she lived for the rest of the year with my brother Arun. Finally, I had the opportunity to observe her interactions with my father's relatives. I began to understand the dynamics at play. In what was clearly a patrilineal family, my father's kin were quite vocal when it came to expressing their gratitude for my father's help. But they were completely oblivious to—or chose to ignore —the sacrifices my mother made along the way. Their attitude was, "What's the big deal? We, too, had to put up with scant resources."

My mother never spoke about this. But I understood what is meant by the adage, "Blood is thicker than water."

The diversion of funds from our immediate family to the foreign relief aid in India meant that our meager domestic budget would be trimmed even further. My mother scrimped hard. She was determined we would eat well and dress at least half-decently. Our home was one of the few with an electric oven, and my mother indulged us with her dazzling cooking skills. She would bake cupcakes which we devoured with our friends. Her samosas were to die for! She even mastered the art of baking British scones.

I was a pre-teen when I started to recognize my mother practiced what she preached. She led her life guided by the scriptures. The fact that she found it difficult to forgive her greedy in-laws shows she is human.

My mother planted the first seeds of spirituality in me and she has been my spiritual guide. When I was young, she shared parables from Hindu epics to guide my thoughts and behaviors. In adulthood, I would use this knowledge to prop me up during challenging times and to ground me during good fortune.

I am no longer surprised when I find photos of deities, cards with inspirational quotes, and small religious mementos in my work desk and bedside cabinet after my mother has visited.

I have witnessed my mother derive enormous strength from her deeply held convictions to face seemingly insurmountable challenges. She would start each day with compassion in her heart and humility in her mind. I hope to emulate her.

One day, when I was about ten years old, I came home from school to find Manjuben, a neighbor's daughter, standing at the front door. She was crying as she waved me to a bedroom down the hall. She did not say anything. I was deeply perplexed. I entered the bedroom and saw my two younger siblings sitting on the bed, looking scared and somber.

Nanu pointed at the bedroom that housed the shrine and said, "*Ba* is not talking."

I crept across the hallway and peered in through the glass door. My mother was lying on the floor in front of the shrine. White frothy liquid poured from her mouth. What had happened? Clearly, she was not well at all. I burst into tears and returned to the bedroom.

The next thing I remember is my father, another gentleman, and Petro carrying my mother in a makeshift stretcher of a bedsheet to our car.

The following seven days or so are a blur. We understood that whatever our mother was sick from was not any ordinary illness. I had never been separated from her except for the rare night for a sleepover at a cousin's. We could not visit her in the hospital. Our elders did their best to reassure us and tried to distract us with treats and activities. But I had lost my appetite. I remember feeling utterly helpless.

At the evening prayers, we fervently prayed for our mother's recovery. Midway through the chanting of prayers, one of us would burst into tears. Then the rest would start sobbing, too. Shobhi tried to comfort us.

A week later, we came home from school at lunchtime and rushed to the kitchen, famished as always. But a family friend who had come to help us redirected us to my mother's bedroom.

Our joy knew no bounds!

Seeing us, my mother burst into tears. We are not a hugging family. But that day, we all hugged and cried together.

For quite a long time afterwards, we would tiptoe around her as if she were a fragile, porcelain doll. We made sure she did not exert herself in any way. We did all the running around for her. At the back of my mind, I feared that one wrong step on my part would send my mother back to the hospital.

I have no doubt that divine intervention, in the form of Manjuben, saved my mother's life. She listened to her sixth sense when she visited my mother on the spur of the moment. Then she cajoled my younger siblings into unlocking the main door which was usually left open during the daytime.

Although much younger than my mother, Manjuben and she were close buddies. They never missed *Navaratri,* the nine nights of dancing preceding the most significant event on the Hindu calendar, Diwali, the festival of lights. Both of them would join the men's circle for vigorous rounds of *Garba.* The ladies' circle was too feeble for them.

It would be several years before I would learn that my mother had taken a bottle of aspirin. The overdose left her hearing permanently impaired. Fortunately, she suffered no other long-term physical consequences.

Over the years, I gathered in bits and pieces that my mother had a serious falling out with my father. Given her deep devotion to religion, she wished to host Shankaracharya Maharaj at our home. Maharaj was head of one of the four major monasteries in India, and he was in Kampala at the time on a lecture tour. If we hosted the Maharaj, our family, friends, and neighbors would get a personal audience with the sage, and our home would be sanctified. It would have been a once-in-a-lifetime opportunity.

I can imagine my father citing financial constraints and leaving no room for negotiation. I wonder if she was going through a depressive episode at the time. Whether my father's denial was the last straw that broke her, I will never know.

Issues like this are not freely discussed in our family. I have never asked my mother about it. Outwardly, she seems to have moved on remarkably well. I assume she harbors ghosts from that somber day. But I like to believe that with the passage of time, her deeply held spiritual convictions, and now having wonderful great-grandchildren, the ghosts no longer haunt her.

I console myself by falling back on what I learned during my psychiatric training.

Sometimes, it is best to leave well enough alone.

But my mother's attempt to take her own life would not be the last word on the subject.

My father: A man of contrasts

My father was born in 1920 in Chakalasi, a tiny potato farming village in northeastern Gujarat, India.

According to the family tree records, his ancestors first settled in the village in 1592. Since then, the birth of every male in the family has been duly recorded in a ledger. Mine is the tenth generation. The records are maintained by a roving registrar of births and deaths who visits the families in the twenty-seven-villages under his jurisdiction twice a year. My father was the youngest of four surviving children. When he was born, his family was unusually small in size because four other siblings died at birth or in their infancy.

When we were growing up, my father frequently told us stories about his childhood. Unlike the stories my mother told us, his tales had little to do with scriptures or religion. He loved contrasting every aspect of life in Uganda with life in India. His comparisons always centered around economics or education.

If one of us complained about the milk, he would say, "When I was growing up, it cost four *annas* (less than a cent) for one *seer* (about two pounds), yet we could not afford it. And here you are making a fuss about it." It did not matter to him that we were not familiar with either the currency or India's ancient commodity weight system.

If we got low grades or preferred to go out and play instead of studying, he would relate to us in great detail his own struggles at a similar age: how he had to complete his homework under the streetlamp because there was no electricity in his village, that he had to walk eight *ghau* (about five miles) each way to and from school. But he never missed school even if the skies opened up with the monsoon's torrential rains or the earth was baking from the scorching heat of the Indian summer. If he was lucky, he would catch a ride on a bullock cart. But that was a rare occasion and public transport was non-existent.

Despite graduating from high school with good grades, my father's education was curtailed. His family, in heavy debt, could not afford to send him to college. His father had mortgaged all his land, partly to support my great-grandfather's opium addiction. The missed opportunity for further education would be his Achilles heel to the end of his days. Single-mindedly, he ensured that it would not be so for any of his children.

In 1938, at only eighteen years old, my father left his beloved India and sailed to East Africa. The only person he knew there was a distant cousin who lived in the landlocked country of Uganda. Within a few days of his arrival, he started working the graveyard shift at a sugarcane factory. He performed multiple tasks, including assisting the bookkeeper. He would do manual labor only as a means to reach his goal—a teaching job.

One bright day in June 1945 in Mombasa, my father walked up a plank to board the *S. S. Karanja,* bound for Bombay. His attire was like that of an Angrez sahib—shorts with braces, knee-high stockings, and a pith hat, the hallmark of British expats at the time. He was in a buoyant mood, not least because he hoped to return to Uganda with a new bride. Seven years earlier when he'd left India for the first time, he swore he would not return until he had repaid every *paisa* of his family's debt. The day had come.

Chakalasi is a part of a rich and powerful community of Patels located in Gujarat, one of the most prosperous states in India. The villages in the area, universally recognized as Charotar, are divided into *gols* (circles) based on a social status hierarchy. *Gols* also serve as endogamous marriage circles.

Chakalasi fell somewhere in the middle of the pack, and it was grouped with the other 26 villages into a *gol* identified as *moti sattavis* or Big 27. It was taboo to marry someone from a lower *gol,* a fantasy to marry someone from a higher *gol,* and unthinkable to marry outside any *gol.*

Today, the younger generations pay scant attention to the *gol* rules when marrying. However, the custom remains deeply rooted. Whether they now live in London or in New Jersey, those of the Charotar diasporas continue to organize themselves along *gol* lines. They meet regularly to celebrate Indian festivals and support each other socially. Matchmaking remains a covert operation.

My father would not have needed a refresher course on the nuances of this age-old custom. He would have been fully cognizant of his limited options to marry.

Upon returning to his village, he likely would have relished receiving the special treatment reserved for foreign-returned sons. He would have been anxious to learn about the matrimonial proposals that he was sure would come from prospective brides' fathers. And he would have been disappointed when they did not materialize. Perhaps his community elders were not impressed with his Ugandan visa. Or perhaps they were unwilling to risk giving away their daughter to the son of a family with a shaky financial past. With his leave running out fast and his bridal prospects dry, his father reluctantly started exploring options outside their *gol.* If necessary, he was willing to forgo the customary practice of collecting a dowry and even pay a bride-price for his son.

Six months after returning home, my father and his oldest nephew were married to my mother and her sister in a double wedding. The wedding was hastily arranged and a clandestine ceremony took place with only a handful of people in attendance. Rumor has it that the match-making middleman pocketed most of the bride-price.

When he returned to Uganda, my father managed to get a job as a primary school teacher. His students would tell us how my father expected them to be proficient in not only calculations involving whole numbers but fractions as well. Those failing to respond promptly were punished with "sir-special"—a pinch of the love-handle hard enough to bring tears to the eyes of even the toughest of the tough cookies.

He soon created a name for himself with his prodigious mathematical brain. He was in great demand as a private tutor. Many parents of children who were either mathematically challenged or needed to be disciplined pleaded with my father to provide tutoring outside the school hours. While coaching on the side would have provided much-needed extra income, my father declined. I was to learn the true reason for his unwillingness many years later.

In 1997, my wife and I visited my primary school teacher, Miss Pramila, at her home in Nairobi, Kenya. She proudly reflected on how my father had resisted the temptation of providing private tutoring to augment his income despite enormous pressure from the community. My father had told her, "I would rather devote every free moment of my time to teaching my own children rather than others."

From the priorities my father set for his children, it was evident he had not forgotten how his own education had been truncated for reasons beyond his control. Now that he was in control, he was determined none of us would share his fate.

Every day, my father would give each one of us maths and English homework appropriate for our age and grade. No study guides or other practice materials were available, so my father would make up the practice examples. After he returned from work in the afternoon and had had his tea, each one of us had to present our completed homework. If we did not meet his high expectations, playtime would be cancelled and we would be given another assignment. This was our home routine on weekdays during the school term for the full duration of seven years of primary schooling. Within a very short time, all of us mastered the subjects to the point that we were doing calculations one or two levels beyond our grade.

All of us, that is, except Nanu, my younger brother.

Delicate Nanu

Nanu was two years younger than me. He had health issues almost from the day he was born. He missed school often and had significant difficulties catching up on his studies. Perhaps his siblings' exceptional performances made his look worse than it really was.

My father decided to give Nanu extra attention to bring him up to par. But his anger would get the better of him. Barely ten minutes into a session, we would hear the sound of a *smack*. From there on, the session would rapidly go downhill. My father's temper would flare, his voice would get louder and mean, and the frequency of smacking would escalate. Sometimes, he would throw the book on the floor. Mercifully for all, that would mark the end of the session.

Peering through the crack left by the hinges of our bedroom door, we would nervously watch. I felt angry with my father, but also hopeless. None of us had the courage to intervene. Today, many would consider my father's behavior tantamount to child abuse.

Poor Nanu, on the other hand, simply could not master the basic arithmetic concepts, hard as he tried. There were days when he was so terrified that he wet himself.

Years later, my father was trying to help my youngest sister, Meeta, with her homework. When he started getting loud, Nanu, who was reading a newspaper in the same room at the time, told Meeta: "Take your book and go to your room. You don't have to take that from him. I have borne it for all of you!"

Score: even!

Education at any cost

Because he lacked credentials beyond a high school diploma, my father could not climb the civil-service ladder. He often used to say, "All I need is a chance." He believed if he could get just one interview, he would dazzle the panel with his knowledge and charm. But no such opportunity came.

Mercifully, his quest for a promotion came to an abrupt end in 1972 when all Asians were expelled from Uganda.

The twin demons of a curtailed education and being forced to marry outside his *gol* hung like a pair of millstones around my father's neck and haunted him throughout his life. He never let us forget this. He made sure none of his children would dream of making education anything but a top priority. He shared his enthusiasm for education with anyone who cared to engage with him. His focus was not limited to schooling. He encouraged us to broaden our horizons by visiting public libraries such as the one run by the United States Information Service. We were never short of reading materials: he subscribed to several weekly and monthly magazines. He joined the local branch of the Theosophical Society and would share some of the discussions with us.

It is hard to fathom how frustrated he must have felt seeing people around him succeed in their careers while his own progress had been halted for want of a piece of paper. I hope he derived some vicarious pleasure from his children's accomplishments.

As for rectifying his other peeve of having his children marry within his *gol*, he was less successful. Only one married within our *gol*, two married into a higher *gol*, and the other three, including me, outside all *gols*.

My father was a man of contrasting colors. On the one hand, he had a fiery temper that would blow at the slightest provocation, and sometimes without any. But the same man could be the heart and soul of a social gathering, entertaining his audience with limitless wit and humor.

The cousin who helped my father immigrate to Uganda lived with his family in a town called Jinja, about fifty miles from Kampala. Jinja is located on the shores of Lake Victoria where the mighty Nile River begins its 4000-mile journey to the Mediterranean Sea. They eagerly awaited my father's monthly visits. After dinner, the hosts, guests, and a few neighbors would gather around him. He would regale them with an endless repertoire of jokes and stories, driving them to hysterical laughter late into the night.

As children, we directly experienced his contrasting sides. If any one of us had less-than-excellent academic grades, our punishment was swift and severe. But if one of us fell ill, my father would quietly worry his head off.

This was the case when my older brother Arun contracted polio. Arun was just one year old when he developed polio which affected his lower limbs. The polio vaccine became available a year later in 1955.

My father left no stone unturned in his search for a remedy. I only came to know about this after reading the meticulously detailed diaries he kept. In the early 1950s, little was known about polio, let alone how to effectively treat it. So it was not surprising that my father took any advice he could get. Much of the advice was well-meaning but far-fetched. Beggars can't be choosers.

Someone told him carrot juice restored power in paralyzed limbs. So it was carrot juice for three straight months for Arun. Someone else said daily enemas would get rid of the poliovirus. My father took it upon himself to administer these to Arun. Fortunately, the torture ended just a week into the experiment when the nozzle of the enema tube got stuck in his rectum. For years before he left for England for further studies, Arun received nightly oil massages at a physiotherapist's home.

I once accompanied my father and Arun to a faith-healing jamboree. The event was highly publicized. Posters boasted a long list of illnesses the faith-healer had reportedly cured. We made our way to the

Nakivubo Stadium in Kampala where we joined a crowd of thousands. There were children and adults with all kinds of disabilities and deformities. I remember feeling scared but also excited. In my child's mind, I visualized Arun cured, walking with a normal gait, as the three of us headed back home after the event.

The crowd patiently waited for several hours and was entertained with traditional dances. Suddenly, a tumultuous roar rose from the crowd. It was a few minutes before I spotted the faith-healer. I think he gave a short sermon. Then he started moving amongst the crowd. He would place his hands for a minute on a child's head and move on to the next child or adult in a row. A few minutes later, several of the people he had touched started jumping in the air, ululating as only Ugandans can. The atmosphere was charged and people were getting excited. We tried to push our way closer to the faith-healer. We were only three or four rows away from him when he turned in the other direction. That is as close as we got. Despondent, we waited for a while before returning home.

With time, my father became more discerning in his efforts to help Arun.

A neighbor's daughter contracted polio about fifteen years after my brother had. Her mother took her to a shaman. The healer applied large amounts of a curd-like substance on the girl's paralyzed legs and wrapped each one in banana leaves. After several days, the girl started complaining about itching and pain. When the healer removed his applications, her limbs were raw, bleeding and denuded of all skin. Only through a surgical miracle were her limbs saved. The girl's mother had invited my brother to join in the treatment, but my father had politely declined. He wanted his son cured, but he was only willing to go so far.

My father rarely showed his emotions. In his diaries, he made no mention of how he felt after each failed treatment. He was optimistic by nature. I am sure his hope for my brother's cure must have sprung eternal. I can only imagine how despondent he must have felt with each failed intervention. Desperation knows no bounds. We have a saying in the Gujarati language: "Only the coconut knows how sweet its water is."

Only my father would have known his pain.

My father's dealings in money-related matters were mystifying. Money was at the root of most of my parent's arguments. Yet he had no qualms funding a couple of classrooms in a new school being built in his village in India. Perhaps that was his way of giving the poor children of his village a chance he did not get. The contradictions in my father's behaviors placed constant stress on our family. It was impossible to predict how he would react to a given situation.

As I look back, I wonder how much of his behavior was at the mercy of the two primordial instincts of hunger and sleep.

He was obsessive about his half-hour power nap after lunch, for which he always came home from his office. He would rush through his meal with comical effect at times. In his haste, he would scald himself trying to quickly drown down hot soup. Then he would complain that my mom was not serving him his food at the right temperature—as if she served meals with a thermometer handy!

Over the weekends, his siesta times would be extended. Before he slept, we would be subject to the same monologue week in and week out —get on with your homework, maintain pin-drop silence, don't go outdoors in the sun. The instructions were explicitly directed at me, but I had no intention of abiding by any of his dictates. On the other hand, we also came to learn that if he slept well, we could be in for an ice cream treat or an outing to Wireless Hill with its majestic view of the city.

Our home in Kampala

I was three years old when my father was transferred to a school in Kampala, the country's capital.

Kampala derives its name from a species of antelopes called impala that once roamed the area in large numbers. Early British colonialists named the area around their settlement "The Hill of the Impala," which translated to *Akasozi ke'Empala* in the local dialect. Eventually, it was shortened to *Kampala* and covered all seven hills the city was originally built on.

The teacher's quarters where we lived were located on the gentle slope of Namirembe Hill, the fourth of Kampala's original seven hills. Our neighborhood was a paradise. The street was fully paved and lined by footpaths on either side. Between the footpaths and the houses, jacaranda trees bloomed. At night, the street was well-illuminated by amber light cascading down from tall wooden light poles. Uganda's equatorial climate guaranteed our narrow boulevard stayed green all year round. On the street itself, hardly any vehicular traffic passed, making it safe for us to play catch ball.

Our bungalow was spacious. It had three bedrooms, a living room, a kitchen with two small pantries across from it, a bathroom, and a nicely screened front verandah. In the corner of one bedroom, we erected a shrine and populated it with photographs of gods, incense stick holders, garlands, and other sanctified objects my mother had brought from her quadrennial visits to India. Just outside the front main door a plant of *tulsi*, holy basil, grew, considered the holiest of plants in India. Gardenia bushes, vines of night-blooming jasmines, Arabian jasmine, and other fragrant plants adorned the front garden.

The houses on the street were built during the British colonial era. So, the solitary toilet was located outdoors like the outhouses in England at the time. While it was only a few steps from the house to the outdoor toilet, crossing that short distance after dark required fathomless courage. You could never be sure who would be lurking around.

The land around our house sloped from the back to the front towards the street. Several large mango trees yielded different varieties of mangoes. Year-round, we were supplied with sweet fruit from the guava tree. Next to it was a large drumstick tree (the Morgina oleifera). Once a year, Petro, under my father's direction, would use a long slender pole to knock down the ripe drumsticks—the long seedpods. It required a delicate flick of the wrist that only Petro could do. My siblings and I would gather the fallen drumsticks and at my mother's direction, we would deliver the bundles to neighbors and friends. In the small piece of land at the back of our house next to Petro's quarters, my father planted cassava, tomatoes, vines of passion fruit, and raspberries. He would be in his element every evening as he inspected his *shambani*.

Adjacent to our house was The Ground. It was the only area on our street big enough for us to play team sports. My brother Arun and I had a complete cricket kit, including coveted Gray-Nicolls bats, and we had a full badminton set as well. Not surprisingly, therefore, The Ground attracted kids from all over the neighborhood. One of our favorite sports was five-a-side cricket, which we played with a tennis ball. There were too many windows nearby to use a real cork and leather cricket ball.

I would like to think I am remembered for my prowess in batting and wicketkeeping on the cricket pitch. But that is not how my brothers and friends remember me. They remember my antics. "Funny in the beginning," they would say, "but tiring with time." When I was struck out, which was often early into the innings, I would take a swipe at the stumps and flatten them in anger. Other times, I would grab the ball in frustration and throw it out of bounds.

Even fifty years later, one of my friend's memories of my antics has not dimmed. A few years ago, he called me. His first words to me were, "Hi, bulldozer!"

The time I spent playing badminton at The Ground, however, had a felicitous end. The sport aroused my interest intensely. No matter how windy the conditions, I would play with whomever I could find. Sure enough, I threw temper tantrums, but mostly I kept them in check out of fear of losing a partner to play against. The hours I spent honing my skills at The Ground would help me win my residence hall championship in India several years later.

When the number of kids got too many, such as during school holidays, we played *gilli danda*. Essentially, it's baseball with sticks. In the version we played, the batter uses a longer stick, *danda*, to hit a small stick, *gilli*, lobbed at him from a short distance. The distance of the hit, measured in walking steps, is the individual's score. The batter stays at bat until he is struck out by failing to connect with the gilli three times in a row or if the hit gilli is caught in flight. Some of the rules of the modern game of cricket owe their origin to this ancient Indian sport.

Another crowd-accommodating sport was *seven stones*. Reportedly played more than 5000 years ago in the Indian subcontinent, it is a game between two teams of "hitters" and "seekers." A hitter tries to knock over a pile of seven stones by throwing a ball. The seekers try to reconstruct the pile, which the hitters try to prevent by striking out the seekers by hitting them with the ball. The only equipment required is a soft ball—and a thick skin!

Kondos

Burglaries were not uncommon when I was growing up. Few neighborhoods were spared. Home alarm systems were unheard of and those without a night watchman, like ours, were particularly vulnerable.

One time, burglars, called *kondos* in Luganda (the language of the Baganda people in Uganda), broke into our house through the bathroom door while we were all sleeping. They had just managed to break in when my father heard them. He woke me up and we turned on all the lights to give the burglars the impression that there were many of us in the house. My father remained near the break-in point at the back of the house while I ran to the screened verandah in the front. Both of us started blowing police whistles we kept handy just for this purpose. We were raising an alarm so that our neighbors could come to our rescue.

After only a few minutes, but what felt like an eon, I saw two figures walk in front of the verandah. Thinking they were neighbors who had come to help, I called out to them. With lightning speed, one of them jumped up the steps and brought down his weapon on the verandah screen with a violent clamor. Then the two ran away.

Once true help arrived, we assessed the damage. The thief had used a cricket stump we had carelessly left outside after play as a weapon. Cricket stumps are made of hard ash wood. Such was the force the thief had used that this one was cracked. Only the steel railing on the verandah screen, and plenty of luck, had saved me that night.

The kondos became more violent with each passing year. The police force was unavailable or ineffective to rein them in, so the people took it upon themselves to deliver justice. A kondo caught stealing, no matter how trivial the loot, would be pelted to death with stones and sticks. I witnessed several such incidents close-up. Each macabre event left me with increasing fear and worsening nightmares.

A few years ago, I was on my way to the airport in Uganda when the vehicle I was in abruptly came to a stop behind a mob that had blocked the road. The driver explained that a kondo was being necklaced, a grim practice in which a rubber tire filled with gas is placed around a person's neck and lit on fire. I did not hear the rest of his commentary, nor did I have the nerve to peer out of the passenger side window.

I still have an occasional nightmare about kondos.

Prayers at the shrine

The people of the Indian diasporas, no matter what part of the world they live in, strive to rigidly adhere to the culture and traditions of their motherland. In Bali, I have seen hundreds of men and women dressed in brightly colored traditional dresses celebrating Holi, the "festival of colors," with pomp and gaiety on their temple grounds. Kigali, Rwanda, is home to only a few hundred Indians, yet they have a shrine with a prayer hall set up in a non-secular building there.

From a very young age, I was taught that every Hindu's home is a temple. Visitors were to be welcomed into the house and not stopped at the threshold. They were to be addressed in the traditional manner using the appropriate, respectful title, offered a seat, and brought a glass of water.

Each individual family relation in Indian society is given a unique title, unlike in many western societies. So while a mother's brother and a father's brother are both *uncles* in the West, in Gujarat, the suffixes -*mama* and -*kaka*, respectively, are added to those uncles' first names when addressing them. Elders are never to be addressed by their first names only.

It didn't take much for me to flagrantly violate this social norm, especially when I had been disciplined by an elder relative or a teacher. I would come home and relate the incident to my mother and my siblings. When I got to the point in my story of naming the disciplinarian, I would use only his or her first name, and I'd add a few mild expletives for crowd effect. My siblings would be amused, but they controlled their merriment so as not to add to my mother's grief. She would shake her head and say, "I pray to God that he hammers some sense into you."

My mother ingrained in us the two fundamentals of Hindu faith: worship of God and meditation. "We meditate to gain mental strength and pray to receive God's blessings," she would say.

During the car ride to school in the mornings, we would pass by our temple. As soon as we approached it, our bickering and bantering would cease, and as if on cue, we would bow our heads and say a few words of prayers. We never needed to be reminded.

In the evenings, we had a more elaborate prayer ritual. Kampala is located only twenty-two miles north of the equator, so days and nights are of equal length throughout the year. The sun always sets around seven in the evening. This was the time for the evening prayers. We would wash our hands and feet and gather at the shrine in our home. There, one of us would light an oil lamp and several incense sticks. Then we would all sing religious songs in chorus.

Om Jai Jagdish Hare is the most common song sung by Hindus at prayer time. While we sang it, one of us would perform the *aarti*, circling the oil lamp in front of the deities in a symbolic offering of light. The song's second verse goes, "*Joh dhyave phal paye*," "Whoever meditates shall obtain the fruit." Thus, the seeds of meditation were planted in my mind in childhood through a devotional song first composed more than five thousand years ago. At the time, I mechanically recited the song with my siblings. I did not yet grasp the meaning or significance of meditation.

Half an hour later, the prayers completed, one of us would take the oil lamp outside and place it under the *tulsi* plant. With divine and devotional duties for the day completed, the Patel household would sit down to a sober vegetarian dinner. Neither meat nor alcohol was ever served in our home.

My parents never joined us in the group prayers. They said their prayers on their own. My father worked the rosary in bed at dawn. My mother would recite mantras and holy passages, and she would sing *bhajans* throughout the day. If she ever sat down to formally pray, I was not aware. I doubt she ever found time to do so with eight mouths to feed. One ritual she maintained without fail, however, occurred at the beginning of the week. Every Monday, she would give me a pint of milk and some fruit to take to the temple to offer to the deities. I would return with *prasad*, blessed food, usually fruits and nuts, for everyone at home.

Hill of tranquility

As we became too old to frolic at The Ground, our location shifted to Museum Hill. A short walk from my home and right across from my secondary school, its actual name was Old Kampala Hill. This was the site where the first British settlers in Uganda had seen herds of impalas roaming and had set up their base. Fort Lugard Museum was the lone building on the hill, hence our pet name for the knoll.

The gently undulating ground there was covered in lush paspalum grass. At one end stood the century-old museum. Opposite it, about one hundred yards away, was a small monument with a flagstaff. The land in between served as a soccer ground, cricket pitch, or for leisurely strolling. On the outskirts were the trenches from wartime, and in the distance were uninterrupted views of the city center.

My most pleasant memories of Museum Hill are of sitting in the shade of the museum building, reading a novel or studying. The sun there was bright and warm, and a cool breeze blew from all directions. Who needed a library when one had such a serene and picturesque place to be?

Today, the hill has been flattened and crowned by a huge, beautiful mosque. Fort Lugard Museum was relocated to a nearby site. But my childhood memory of Museum Hill is as fresh as a Ugandan gerbera daisy.

Coming of the Last King of Scotland

"Where do you think you mother-foxers are going?" the army soldier yelled.

The streets of Kampala were unusually quiet that morning as my father and I drove to work. I was fifteen years old and working a summer job as an accounts clerk in my father's office. My father was telling me that he had not slept well because of the ceaseless gunfire throughout the night. I, too, had heard a lot of noise but did not know it was gunfire. I had never before heard a live firearm discharge.

A unit of army barracks was stationed on a hill a mile from our house. My father surmised that the local police must have joined forces with the army to crack down on kondos. Gangs of these thieves roamed the streets of Kampala at night, breaking into private residences and looting whatever they could get their hands on. They severely beat or even slaughtered with a machete those who resisted them.

"The law and order situation has gone way south," my father said. He added, "It is time for some action."

There had been no news related to Uganda on the BBC that morning. If the most authentic news agency in the world had nothing to report, we had nothing to worry about. Everything was under control. It would be safe to drive to work.

Driving along, we were struck by the scant traffic on the streets. Shops were shuttered and their owners milled outside in small groups.

As we passed by the nation's parliament building, I saw a soldier in full fatigues carrying a machine gun run down the steps, waving at us to stop. My father had been distracted by something on the other side of the road and did not see him. I yelled at my father to stop the car. He braked hard.

The soldier shoved his machine gun through the passenger side window, right in front of my face, and held it an inch from my father's temple and let out another expletive. His eyes were bloodshot. He was panting and sweating profusely despite the cool, early morning air—probably more from an adrenaline rush than the physical exertion of running the twenty yards or so to where we had come to a stop.

I hastily mumbled an apology in utter dread. "Sorry... sorry, *bwana*... sorry...," I said. I did not know what I was apologizing for. I was just hoping he would not fire. I tried to make friendly eye contact with him. But he stared intently at my father. By this time, my father seemed to have recovered from the initial shock. He politely informed the soldier that we were headed to work at the Ministry of Education headquarters just up the road.

If my father felt the gravity of the situation, he never let on one bit.

I will never know what saved us that day. Perhaps it was because my father said we worked for the government. Perhaps it was his cool response. Perhaps the soldier had orders not to shoot. Probably it was a combination of all of the above plus a lot of divine intervention. Whatever the reason, our fate that day was one of reprieve.

After the few minutes that felt like an eternity, the soldier let out yet another expletive and ordered us to turn around.

My father made a quick U-turn. We had driven barely a hundred yards when an army tank came straight at us. My father swerved into a side street in the nick of time. Using back streets, we made our way home.

That was enough excitement to last a lifetime.

It would be several hours before we would hear on the BBC that the Ugandan government had been toppled in a coup by the army. The date was January 25, 1971. Idi Amin, the "Last King of Scotland," had arrived and begun his tyrannical reign.

My father's life would never be the same again.

Inspirational Kanubhai

My godmother's eldest son, Kanubhai, lived with us during most of my childhood. Such an arrangement was common then. Boarding and lodging facilities for single men were few. Even if a suitable one were to be found, my parents would have never allowed their best friend's son to live anywhere else.

Kanubhai was handsome, charismatic, and sharp-witted. He was about fifteen years older than me and worked as a teacher at the Kibuli Secondary School, just outside Kampala. It was no wonder he was so popular with his students. He would purchase stationery for them from the Patel Press, the city's premier bookstore, and give them rides into the city or to the hospital.

At home, he was equally sought after. My mother and her friends would patiently wait for him to return from school late Saturday morning. They would bundle into his Baby Fiat and head to the local Nakasero market for the week's shopping of fruits and vegetables, make social visits, or visit someone in the Mulago Hospital. Kanubhai's services were indispensable and his charm made the cramped rides bearable.

Kanubhai took an active interest in us kids. His priorities for us were studies, sports, sightseeing, sartorial splendor, and style—in that order. My two older siblings were happy to toe the line. But I can't say the same for myself.

One of Kanubhai's pet peeves was long hair. In the 1960s, The Beatles were becoming popular, and impressionable boys like me took active notice of their fashionably long hair. Not Kanubhai, though. His idea of an acceptable length of hair for boys was scalp-short.

Arun and I would be sent off to the local barber with explicit instructions to get a "Korean" cut. Even at the tender age of ten years, I was fast becoming conscious of my physical appearance. I was constantly teased for the *chotli*, cowlick, that stubbornly stood on the back of my head. Copious quantities of castor oil failed to subdue it. There was no way I was going to have my hair cut short.

Once after I returned with my version of a Korean cut, Kanubhai asked me when I was going to get a haircut. I showed him my freshly shaved nape as evidence that I had just had one. He was not amused.

But the barber was. I was his first customer ever to have two haircuts on the same day.

One day when I was about 15 or 16, I bitterly complained about our family friend-cum tailor. I blamed him for using cheap material because my trousers were shrinking after each wash! Barely a few months would pass and my socks would start showing. Kanubhai said nothing and gave that all-knowing smile of his.

Of course, it never occurred to me that I was going through an exceptionally fast growth spurt. I must have grown six inches in a year. Or at least that's the story my trousers told.

Sorrowful Jaya

My siblings and I were the beneficiaries of Kanubhai's keen interest in travelling and sightseeing. After ensuring we had completed our homework and extra lessons, we would embark on a day trip to the botanical gardens and the zoo at Entebbe on the shores of Lake Victoria. We would leave home in the early morning, spend the day swimming in the lake, walk around the beautiful gardens, have a picnic, and most joyfully, spend the last hour at the zoo before returning home bone tired.

During one school holiday, we took a memorable four-day trip to Murchison Falls National Park. Located in the northwest part of the country, the mighty Victoria Nile gushes through a mere 23-foot-wide gap to create the majestic Murchison Falls. In the 1960s, the park teemed with hordes of elephants, buffalos, rhinos, Ugandan kobs, and many other species of wild animals and birds before the civil wars and large-scale poaching decimated their populations. Needless to say, in the weeks before our trip, all the talk amongst ourselves was about the wildlife we would see and how close to the falls we would get.

Finally, the day arrived. In the tradition of most Indian families, we made our mandatory visit to the temple before embarking on our trip. As soon as I stepped out of the car, I saw my classmate, Jaya, sitting outside on the temple steps. Jaya was a small, malnourished girl who came from a very poor family. Her school uniform was always tattered and she never had money to buy books or pencils. Our big-hearted class teacher, Miss Pramila, would often send one of us to buy *mogo* for Jaya from the school canteen during recess. Quite often, this would be the only meal she would have all day.

So when I saw her, I felt very sad. Here I was all excited about a trip while this poor girl was starving. I don't remember if I prayed for her, but that incident left a lasting impression. Since that day, I have always made a conscious effort not to show any overt excitement before going on a trip. While my efforts to subdue any anticipation changed a little after my daughter was born, Jaya's image remains steadfastly imprinted on my mind.

Farewell Uganda

My fourteen years in Kampala were coming to an end.

My father's motto, "Education at any cost," was being extended to "and further education anywhere in the world."

Whenever one of us did not perform to his expectation, my father's favorite threat was, "I will ship you off to Chakalasi and you can toil on the farm."

My pet response was, "I would never go to India. Uganda is my home."

Not one to give up, he would say, "Well, in which case you can graze Kabaka's goats."

I am sure the King of Buganda, the province we lived in, would have been happy to get free labor!

My father's uncompromising stand on education, without doubt, laid the foundation for all our siblings' careers. And Kanubhai, who had studied commerce in India, was a big help with his vast knowledge of the educational systems in India and the UK. His thoughtful assessments of our academic strengths and weaknesses and his understanding of my father's limited finances yielded life-changing solutions for our family.

Since I wished to study medicine, Kanubhai felt that a college in India would be the best option because tuition there was affordable. My two older siblings were already studying in the UK, and my father could not afford to support another one there.

By this time, Kanubhai had left his teaching job to work as an accountant at a prestigious road building company. Despite his busy work schedule and raising his own young family, he found time to write to colleges in India and network with his medical friends, Madhuben and Jagoobhai, on my behalf.

So with the help of the doctor couple's relatives in India, I was able to get a place at the Ahmedabad Science College in Ahmedabad. I would be joining thousands of students all over Gujarat vying for the precious few seats in medicine.

One bright afternoon in August 1972, as a cool breeze blew in from Lake Victoria, I made my way up the ramp stairs to board the Air India flight from Entebbe to Bombay. Halfway up the stairs, I looked back at the gallery, searching for my family. I was barely able to hold back my tears as an air hostess showed me to my seat. The only one in my family who said he would never go to India for his studies was headed there!

1.2 – The Patel siblings, 1994:
Nanu, Shirish, Shobhi, Arun, Meeta, Mayoor

The beautiful country of my birth was not the only thing I was leaving behind. I had developed a crush on my neighbor's daughter. Under the pretext of getting my help with her studies, she would come to our house, and we would chit-chat about nothing in particular. Our heartstrings would strain when we would part, and both of us always looked forward to our next meeting. Our brief platonic relationship came to an abrupt end when I left for India.

Just a few weeks after my departure, President Idi Amin would issue a decree expelling all Asians from Uganda.

A despot, Amin was also a colorful character who bestowed upon himself various decorations. At the height of his power, his title was His Excellency, President for Life, Field Marshal Al Hadji Doctor Idi Amin Dada, VC, DSO, MC, Lord of All the Beasts of the Earth and Fishes of the Seas and Conqueror of the British Empire in Africa in General and

Uganda in Particular. To top it all, he claimed to be the uncrowned sovereign head of Scotland. That claim lent the name to his biopic, *The Last King of Scotland*.

Two: Studies In India

1972-1980

I resolve to be mindful of the nature of my work. I will do only what is ethical and productive, and what does not violate my values and principles.

—from Swami Tyagananda's
Walking the Walk: A Karma Yoga Manual

An undergrad in Ahmedabad

A hmedabad is the largest city in Gujarat. The Sabarmati River weaves its way through the city and is probably best known for the ashram of the same name, a monastic community that Mahatma Gandhi set up on its bank in 1917.

Being in Ahmedabad was like being in another world. Every street teemed with people on the move. In Kampala, if you saw five people together, it was a crowd. More than three cars on our street, and we would consider it a traffic jam. But in Ahmedabad, an endless procession of bicycles, rickshaws, scooters, cars, and buses rushed by, seemingly all honking at the same time. Stray dogs, wandering cows, and the occasional camel cart added to the clamor and the color. The cacophony of modern India was painfully disorienting to my young ears.

It took me a long time to find my rhythm in this city of organized chaos. The location of my college—smack in the middle of the old city —did not help matters.

During my first year there, I survived a bout of malaria and multiple episodes of dysentery. When I went to a tailor to have the waistband of my trousers taken in, he asked me in all sincerity if the trousers were a hand-me-down from my father! I had lost about thirty pounds. Just when I thought the worst was behind me, I came down with a severe attack of chickenpox. My torso was covered in the tell-tale rash which matured into pustules over a week. Itchy, feverish, and thoroughly miserable in the summer heat, I lay in bed, worrying. Would the whole purpose of my coming to India come to naught?

With my final exams barely a month away, my paternal aunt and my sister-in-law nursed me back to health. They brewed different traditional concoctions to help me regain my strength and took turns maintaining vigil just outside my bedroom.

Med school in Baroda

The chickenpox attack left me exhausted. Somehow, I managed to sit for my finals.

I took an additional open test a few months later in Baroda (now Vadodara). Science students from colleges all over Gujarat took this test to try to grab one of the coveted seats in medicine at the prestigious Medical College, Baroda. I was thrilled when I had offers from both Ahmedabad and Baroda. Choosing which to take was easy. Medical College, Baroda, had a fantastic reputation, and my godmother had moved to Baroda from her village.

Maharaja Sayajirao University, named after the last ruler of Baroda, is a residential university. The faculty buildings with their unique domes and arches stand out in a sea of concrete jungle. The student residence halls are located on grounds spacious enough to play volleyball and tennis-ball cricket. Students come from all corners of India and neighboring countries. If one so chose, one could have national and international cultural experiences without ever leaving the campus.

I had cleared the first hurdle of getting into a medical school. While there would be many more hurdles to clear, for now, life felt as refreshing as a cool breeze on an Indian summer day.

The burana gang

At the end of an English lecture in pre-med class, a student sitting next to me on the last bench asked me if my roommate, Raju Patel, was from Karamsad. The village is famous as the hometown of Sardar Vallbhbhai Patel, a freedom fighter and India's first deputy prime minister.

I had been periodically glancing at him as he napped throughout the period, his head buried in his crossed arms on the desk.

I replied in the affirmative as he introduced himself as Nitin Patel.

Though Nitin, Raju, and I share the same last name, we are not blood-related. The surname *Patel* is common in Gujarat. Perhaps centuries ago, our ancestors came from the same geographical area and retained their last name as they dispersed across the country and the globe.

Nitin was a short, slim guy with curly hair and a hurried walk. What he lacked in stature, he made up in his oration, especially in the tone of authority that accompanied his words.

He was born and spent his early childhood in Nairobi, Kenya, before moving with his mother and two brothers to their village, Karamsad, in India. His father remained behind in Kenya. This was not an unusual arrangement after African countries started gaining independence. The future of Asians in ex-colonies was becoming precarious, and India offered a safe haven.

The Indian students from East African countries of Uganda, Kenya, and Tanzania hung around together. Local students referred to us as *bwana,* an honorific Swahili title. We used the word frequently in daily conversation, akin to the way Australians use the word, *mate. Bwanas* often roomed amongst themselves, patronized fancy restaurants, wore Levis, and preferred private transport in rickshaws over buses—all made possible by generous remittances sent from parents abroad. As a group, our focus was on the finer aspects of life: studying was definitely not one of them. We were birds of a feather flocking together and over-egging the pudding.

When we were not playing hooky, our goal was to find a way to get classes cancelled. One of our biochemistry professors offered an easy target. The cantankerous gentleman was biding his time until retirement. He had an exceptionally low threshold for any kind of noise while he was teaching. The slightest disturbance would set him off and he would threaten us with all kinds of reprisals. His class routine was to first read us the riot act, and then he would start scribbling on the blackboard. One day, no sooner had he turned his back to the class, when Nitin, sitting right next to me, loudly stamped his feet on the wooden floor three or four times in rapid succession.

2.1 – Me and Nitin, 1984

I was petrified, as was the rest of the class.

The professor slowly turned around and stared at the class for a long moment. Unable to identify the culprit, he pointed to the most visible member of our class, a Sikh student wearing a turban, and yelled, "Sardarji, get out of the class!"

The young man slowly stood up and protested it was not him. He was sitting a few seats away from us and knew who the offender was, but admirably, even as the whole class was expelled, he did not snitch on Nitin.

Sometimes the bwanas would carry their cavalier practices to the extreme. Once, Nitin decided to take a break from the first semester of medical school to carouse in Kenya. When he returned three months later, he had almost doubled in size. This made some of the clinically astute students in our class speculate that he had anasarca—a generalized swelling of the body caused by a medical condition like liver failure. "Very possible, considering all the beers you drank there," we would rub it in. Yet, living in the dry state of Gujarat, we wished we could have joined him for a cold Tusker, the famous Kenyan beer.

After finishing medical school, Nitin went to Kenya, and I left for Zambia. Two years later, our paths would cross again. Once again, our goals would be aligned, and we would both take a very different approach this time.

"Hi! I am Harish Vishram. But they call me Harry. Dirty Harry, ha ha ha!" said a tall, handsome, bearded gentleman as he extended his hand to me. Dressed in a white kurta and Levis, Harry was an engineering student who would be rooming with Raju, my medical school partner, and me. With Nitin, his arrival rounded off our gang of four.

Harry was born and raised in Zimbabwe. Unlike Raju and I, he was entirely at home whether he was at a five-star restaurant ordering from an inch-thick menu or in a student's mess with an oral menu. He could speak with equal ease to a CEO or the campus bicycle repairer. To Harry, no one was too superior to be worshipped or too inferior to be ignored.

Harry was deeply religious. One of the first things he did after joining us was to set up a shrine in a corner of the covered balcony at the back of our dorm room. There he would start his day with morning prayers and light a lamp before going to class. He was not at all bashful in performing *pujas*, rituals traditionally conducted by female members of the family.

He had grown up in a highly westernized environment. His Gujarati was as sketchy as his English was fluent. But this did not deter him from singing *bhajans* in Sanskrit. He took classes to learn to play sitar. Sometimes, he would practice for hours accompanied by singing in different *ragas*. I only know this because he explained them to me. I could not tell one end of classical Indian music from the other.

Harry and Raju kindled my interest in music. Raju owned a tape recorder and numerous Bollywood music cassettes of the evergreen eras from the 1950s to 1970s. Late into the night, we all would listen to melodies belted out by Lata Mangeskar, the nightingale of Indian music, her sister, Asha Bhosle, and male singers like Mohammed Rafi and Mukesh. Even today, I can listen to them perpetually. Anytime my mood takes a dip, Lataji's voice lifts me up. Perhaps it's a childish fantasy, but in my reincarnation, my only prayer is that I retain fondness for Hindi music.

Harry was a strict vegetarian, a teetotaler, and a non-smoker. Nitin, Raju, and I indulged in all three vices. But Harry rarely criticized our ways or tried to change us. He was comfortable in his skin. His character had been smoothly molded by a mix of eastern and western cultures, practices, and habits, like a glass marble's blend of aesthetic colors.

Privileged professors, privileged med students

In the 1970s, Medical College, Baroda and its affiliate, Sir Sayajirao General Hospital, were elegant edifices, albeit inadequately equipped. The hospital, as the largest civil facility in the area, was always teeming with people suffering from all kinds of maladies, from heat, and from noise pollution generated by a thousand honking rickshaws.

Across the lane from the main entrance to the college was a small, beautiful temple. This house of God was especially busy at exam times as the medical students petitioned the Almighty for passing grades. Our dorm was only a short walk away. Conveniently located along the way were street vending carts selling *paan* (betel quid), *gutka* (chewing tobacco), and cigarettes. Vices for sure, but they helped mitigate the suffering.

In the early 1970s, the influence of The Monkees was prevalent in India. Guys wore bell-bottoms and kept their hair long—but not medical students. As budding doctors, we had to lead by example. Or so said our anatomy professors. They shamelessly picked on young men who had not visited a barber in a while or had an avant-garde tailor.

These lab kings would encourage questions during the cadaver dissections and then chastise us for asking "dumb" questions. It was not like we did not know arteries from veins and nerves, but many muscles did look alike to our first year-medical-student eyes. Rumor had it that many of the anatomy professors failed to make it in the clinical world and had thus ended up in academia. If true, their displaced frustration was on full display.

But the biggest egos were on the clinical side.

Dr. Adit Iyangar, a senior medical consultant, had one of them. When his chauffeur-driven car pulled up at the hospital entrance, he expected his entourage of junior staff to be waiting for him. In ascending order of seniority, one would open the car door, another would carry his attaché, and the senior registrar would escort him to the ward. The rest of the entourage would dutifully follow.

Once in a while, he would ask one of us to present a case. On a good day, he was an excellent teacher. On a bad day, he would spend time dressing down the perceived truants amongst us. The unfortunate ones were identified by his senior registrar in a completely random and arbitrary manner. None of us would ever dream of challenging our consultants: the result would be an automatic failure in the subject. Some brave students found that out the hard way. Almost thirty years after India's independence, the snobbery of the British Raj of superior *sahib* and lowly *gulam* (boss and servant) mentality was still very much prevalent. Only now, the sahib and the gulam were both Indians.

Then there was Dr. Kamuk. He was a senior trainee—not a full-fledged consultant. But he seemed to derive sadistic pleasure from literally tearing up medical histories he felt did not meet his standards. All the long hours we had spent charting a patient's medical history would be shredded to bits in a few seconds. We were never able to figure out his standards because he changed them more often than he changed his white coat. All we could do was patiently wait for our rotation with him to end.

Several years later in Zambia, I encountered Indian-trained consultants who would also expect us junior doctors to be subservient. "Yes sir, no sir, three bags full, sir!"

While we had several professors who were kind and respectful, they were few and far between. I have never been able to fathom what drives people to behave towards others in such a belittling way. Our professors were all highly learned and in many cases trained in the UK. They could have easily spent their time imparting some of their vast knowledge to us, especially since we had to rely on good clinical acumen to diagnose an illness in that era. We did not have access to sophisticated laboratories or medical imaging facilities as we do today.

"I think it is the result of the Indian heat and *garam masala*," a friend once facetiously opined.

I think their behaviors were driven by narcissism.

In India, medical students are idolized. Outside the hospital campus, it was not at all unusual to see a medical student with his stethoscope hung around his neck or prominently displayed in his breast pocket. This symbol of the healing profession opened up doors not otherwise accessible to ordinary mortals. Movie tickets for house-full shows suddenly became available. Restaurants proffered choice seats.

Perhaps this privilege explains the behavior of our professors. The seeds of narcissism were probably planted in them from the time they entered medical school.

Possibly as an antidote to the stress of professors' demands and the program's rigors, many of my classmates pursued practical jokes and humor as an escape. So, whatever many of our professors lacked in humor, my classmates more than made up for it.

As a group of cerebral students in our class couldn't figure out how a lobe of the brain ended up in their cadaver's abdominal cavity, the culprits snickered behind their backs.

A donnish young woman became a target of joking. She would spend an inordinate amount of time viewing slides. Once, we were lined up to view a slide of kidney tissue. The histology of this organ is quite easy to recognize. The hallmark feature of the glomerulus appears as a large circle surrounded by thousands of cells, which appear as small dots. The time to view the slide should have been quickly completed by each student. Not for this young woman. Suddenly, I felt a tap on my shoulder, and in a voice loud enough for her to hear, Bhartendu Mehta said to me, "You don't have to count the cells, do you?" The young woman turned around from the microscope and gave us a killer stare. But the quip was too good for me to be able to stifle my laughter!

I found oral exams particularly stressful. I intensely feared either freezing up or giving an outrageous answer. I have a tendency to talk very fast, which meant I was asked even more questions than if I would have spoken slowly or methodically. But this insight would not come to me until much later.

Once before radiology orals, I was sitting with my batch mates who were discussing possible questions we would face. As I listened, my anxiety started escalating. I got up and took a solitary stroll down the hallway. I focused on my slow, deliberate steps, counting them. I must have been doing this for about five minutes when my name was called out.

I performed well in the orals. But more importantly, I distinctly remember feeling calm and focused. I now believe that was the day I took my first step (pun unintended) into meditation.

In February 1980, I completed my year-long mandatory medical internship.

My goal was to pursue advanced training in the UK. But I needed to clock extra hours of internship before I could sit for the British licensing examination. Arun was on a contract in Zambia and the lure of returning to Africa and being closer to my brother was too great to resist. A few weeks after completing my internship in India, I left for the central African country with a two-day stopover in the Indian Ocean island of Mauritius.

My seven-year stay in India had come to an end. My life as a real doctor was about to begin. I was happy to leave behind the stifling heat and the high-octane atmosphere of medical school. Things could only get better hereon.

Or so I thought.

Three:
Doctoring in Zambia
1980-1982

I resolve to be mindful of the quality of my work. I will work with love and care, remembering that my happiness depends on it.

—from Swami Tyagananda's
Walking the Walk: A Karma Yoga Manual

University Teaching Hospital:
A cold sandwich, a warm Coke

The climate of Zambia is significantly more moderate than India's. The country is sparsely populated. And as for the air and water, what can I say? It is Africa at its best! I was home.

I was employed at the University Teaching Hospital in the capital city of Lusaka. As the biggest public hospital in the country, it attracted patients from near and far. Villagers would come with their entire families and cook and sleep on the hospital grounds while waiting for the recovery of their loved ones who slept on one of the hospital's 1500 beds.

As a junior house officer, I was the lowest on the medical totem pole. On paper, I was a trainee. But in reality, I was expected to perform like an independent doctor. The patient flow left little time to receive supervision, to attend grand rounds or any other form of continuing medical education. I learnt through osmosis and made sure that I did not repeat my mistakes. I relied heavily on my textbook knowledge, which was noteworthy. Yet my practical experience was not worthy of mention. So whenever it came to performing procedures such as taking a biopsy or applying casts, I prayed hard.

The pace of work was frenetic. If I was not working, I was sleeping, and vice versa. My colleagues were doing the same. I came to accept this chaos as the new norm. Memories of the luxurious life I had as a medical student quickly faded.

On my very first day on call in the pediatric unit, I was whisked away for a quick "lunch" at four in the morning.

Since eight o'clock the previous morning, I had been busy admitting young children bloated from *kwashiorkor*—a form of severe protein malnutrition—almost comatose from malaria, and severely dehydrated from diarrhea and vomiting caused by gastroenteritis. On the unit, it was a one-person show. You admitted the babies, drew their blood samples, prescribed their medications, and started the IV drips. The latter would take forever unless you were lucky to access a collapsed vein. For every child I tucked in, it seemed three others had taken his or her place. Could the clock hands sweep faster and bring my shift to a merciful end?

The senior charge nurse who had seen many newbies like me pass through her unit took pity on me. She probably figured that a half-fed, half-dead doc was better than no doc. She locked me in the staff room where I gulped down a cold sandwich and a warm coke.

By the time I left my twenty-four-hour shift the following morning, I had pronounced eight babies dead. I don't remember meeting any of the grieving mothers or consoling them. I do remember feeling bone-tired and utterly numb as I walked to the parking lot.

By the end of my first week on duty, I had worked more than one hundred hours. And the rest I had slept.

During rare quiet moments on the pediatric unit, I would fantasize about providing toys, books, and a zillion other things to make the kids happy. The distress of the children in the burns unit was difficult to cope with. They would lie listlessly or wail in their cribs all day long with no toys to take their minds away from their suffering.

Gradually, I learnt several self-survival techniques. Informal group therapy in the doctor's lounge and occasional visits to a disco club helped a great deal to relieve the stress. So did a few pints of Mosi, Zambia's iconic beer, at the local Pamodzi Hotel. I think every intern's duty should include at least a few hours a week of dedicated time at a watering hole!

Life as an intern was becoming bearable—with the exception of the high rate of patient mortality.

Patient with cancer

During my general medicine rotation, I had a patient with terminal cancer under my care. Aware that his prognosis was poor, Boniface

Madegwa made few medical demands and spent most of his time in bed. He came from a prominent family and stayed in our unit for several months. Palliative care was unheard of at the time. During our daily rounds, and whenever I had some free time, I would stop by his bedside to chit chat. Soon both of us looked forward to the visits.

One Sunday evening, as I was returning to my accommodation located on the hospital grounds, a nurse told me Boniface had passed away. She said that near the end of his time, he repeatedly asked for me. I became quite upset. We had developed a friendly bond. I sought consolation from a colleague, Ranjana Parmar, who calmly rebuked me: "You should never get emotionally close to a patient."

When I reflected on Boniface's death, I surmised he would have been petrified of his impending demise. That was to be expected. The two weeks of psychiatric training I had received during medical school had not prepared me to do any kind of patient counseling.

As a newly-minted doctor, my vision was limited to viewing patients through medical lenses only. If a medical remedy were available, I would deliver it. Anything outside the field of medicine was not within my purview. Boniface and I had talked about the treatment of his bedsores and ways of stimulating his appetite but never about his feelings or his fear of death. I had yet to learn to fathom death in patients under my care. I knew I had to learn to look beyond the limitations of science.

A teacher at medical school had once vaguely mentioned the value of the defense mechanism of intellectualization for doctors. She explained it would help us avoid uncomfortable emotions if we remained focused on scientific facts. According to her, then, I should have thought about Boniface's case only in terms of cancer cells: cancer cells are invasive; they overwhelm the body's defense systems; there are a wide variety of therapeutic options, and the mortality rate is high.

That is a useful lens to look through, perhaps. But it is merely medical jargon trying to shield the heart.

The kiosk vendor

In Zambia, I made several lifelong friends, and we managed to even get away for a few days to Kafue National Park. I had enlightening experiences in the most unexpected of places and from the most ordinary of souls.

One day at a cricket match, I purchased a soft drink at a kiosk. The gentleman did not have the right amount of change. It was a matter of only twenty *ngwee*, a few cents, but I held my ground. Without the slightest bitterness, he rounded off the cost to the nearest whole figure and handed me more money than I was owed. Before I could say anything, he smiled and said, "Some you win, some I win."

What magnanimity that gentleman had! After toiling in the heat all day long, earning a fraction of what I did, he had the composure to deal with a tightwad with a smile. He was a winner who saw winners in others, too. From his perspective, no one had to be a loser.

A heartbreaking loss

"Shirish, could you please step out for a minute?" a friend of my brother's asked.

I had been relaxing with a colleague at his place one evening after a hectic on-call night. I did not have time to even hazard a guess what his request was about when his next words took the wind out of my sails.

"Your father passed away early today."

I don't remember much after that. I remember going back into the house. My world started spinning. I collapsed on the sofa, buried my head in a cushion, and sobbed uncontrollably.

My father lived with Arun in England. He had woken up gasping for air as he came down the stairs. The family doctor was summoned and he immediately ordered an ambulance. As my father was being loaded onto the ambulance, he asked my brother for his footwear. Those were his last words. My brother and my mother followed the ambulance in his car. A few minutes into the ride, the ambulance turned on its flashing lights and siren.

"That was when my heart sank," Arun later recalled.

More than an hour after he was wheeled into the emergency room, a teary-eyed nurse came out into the waiting room. She broke the news to my mother and brother: my father had died of a massive heart attack. He was 60 years old.

Encountering death in a patient and death in a family member are experiences a world apart. Intellectualization works well in the former, but it has little redemption value in the latter.

The doctor in me tried to understand my father's death in terms of his obesity, hypertension, and smoking habit. But simultaneously, the son in me refused to accept these reasons. My father never touched a drop of alcohol in his life. He was a strict vegetarian. Even more importantly, he led an honest life dedicated to his family and his community.

I am convinced the premature retirement forced on my father by President Idi Amin's expulsion of all Asians from Uganda in 1972 was a watershed event in his life. In Uganda, he had a job. Employment brought with it dignity and respect. He had a purpose in life. But all of that was suddenly taken away. He was not given a chance to plan his retirement. After 34 years of hard work, he did not get a chance to determine how he would spend the twilight years of his career. In the UK, he could not find a job. My father had prided himself on self-sufficiency all his life, and he was reduced to collecting unemployment benefits. Over the next eight years, life slowly seeped out of him.

The most painful part of his demise was that his children were just getting ready to assume the role of carer and provider. But we would not get that privilege. Our ship had lost its captain. For a long time, we felt like we were on a rudderless ship until Arun, the most fully-fledged amongst us, took over the wheel and steered our family back on course.

On my father's first death anniversary, I woke up at dawn and drove to the Hindu temple in the city. As I sat on the floor facing the statues of Indian deities, my mind became strangely devoid of all thoughts. I felt at complete peace. The experience could not have lasted more than a minute, but I felt as if my father had joined me in that brief moment.

There is much to be said about the sanctity and the serenity offered by a place of worship.

Bodies die, not the Self that dwells therein.

—from *The Bhagavad Gita*,
trans. by Eknath Easwaran

My original plan was to spend only six months in Zambia to obtain the necessary credits that would allow me to sit for the UK licensing exam. But six months had magically rolled into eighteen. It was time to get back on track.

Four:
Philosophical & Personal Growth in the UK
1982–1988

I resolve to be mindful of the approach to my work. I will do my work as work for work's sake expecting no rewards, seeking no favors, and avoiding no challenges.

—from Swami Tyagananda's
Walking the Walk: A Karma Yoga Manual

Three pork chops

T hree pork chops," shouted a gang of white guys from across the road as Arun, a friend, and I made our way to a pub in the evening in downtown Winchester, a beautiful cathedral city in southeast England. The year was 1974. It was my first visit to the UK, where my parents and younger siblings had been absorbed by the British government as a part of the 27,000 Asians expelled from Uganda.

A few weeks before, on a visit to the seaside resort of Blackpool in northwest England, the three of us had to spend a night in a parking lot. Making a prior reservation was not standard practice then. One expected to easily find a place for the night amongst the hundreds of bed and breakfast inns that lined the shores of the Irish Sea coast. But we had no such luck. We knocked on the doors of one inn after another. "Sorry, we have no vacancy," was the consistent response. Yet we observed there always was room at the inn for a white patron.

I had heard and read about racial discrimination, but this was my first time experiencing it personally—if you don't count the time in Kampala when I was about eight or nine years old. A white man handed a shilling to my lighter-colored friend, saying, "This is for you." Though he inserted a few coins into the donation jar I was carrying, he was otherwise oblivious to my existence. He briskly walked away, saying no words and making no eye contact with me. I was too young to make any connection between the man's action and the color of my skin.

Eight years after that night in the Blackpool parking lot, I returned to England for my residency training. I found little had changed in the arena of xenophobia.

Once, Ranjana (my colleague from Zambia), her husband Prakash, and I went to a pub for a beer in Scarborough, the town made famous by Simon and Garfunkel's song "Are You Going to Scarborough Fair." As we pulled into the parking lot, the bartender came out and started gesturing at us, staving us off. The same bartender showed no qualms, at least not outwardly, of serving me when I was accompanied by a white friend a few days later.

Initially, I only picked up on overtly racist behaviors. As I became more sensitive to the issue, I started noticing acts of covert prejudice as well.

One evening at badminton club at the hospital, I put my name down on the roster and took a seat on a bleacher. The procedure was that the person whose name appeared on the top of the list would inform the next three what court they would play on. When my turn came, the person whose name was before mine calmly skipped calling me and selected the three after me. She happened to be a student nurse rotating through our unit at the time and had interacted with me on several occasions. But outside the hospital, she would not indicate any recognition of our acquaintance. I guess "playing the white man" (as the British used to say to indicate "doing the right thing") was not part of her repertoire!

I quickly learnt that my British passport did not guarantee me acceptance into their society. I was judged by the color of my skin. I began to avoid situations that would put me in uncomfortable social interactions. So, if I were alone and wanted to go out for a meal, I would go to an Indian restaurant or get a take-out. I frequented Asian clubs. While they lacked the décor and ambience of British pubs, at least I was welcome there. And they were unlikely to trigger any symptoms of post-traumatic stress disorder!

I believe xenophobic behaviors are most unfortunate. They color (pun unintended) one's vision and truncate an individual's cultural, spiritual, and aesthetic growth. In the end, everybody loses, and nobody is any the wiser.

My wife Shashi and I were once vacationing in the beautiful Lake District in Cumbria, northwestern England. It boasts scenic ribbon lakes, rolling mountains, and small market towns which dot the area. It was a busy long weekend, but we were lucky to secure a bed and breakfast with an English couple. When we arrived at the lodging, the landlady greeted us. As we entered her home, she said little and kept looking at my wife. My paranoid mind started thinking that she was expecting a white couple and was shocked to see Indians instead. But my paranoia was short-lived. Pointing at a photograph on the fireplace mantel, she remarked how similar my wife looked to her daughter-in-law, who was also Indian.

And then there was the time some white kids yelled at us as we passed them while crossing the Peace Bridge over the Niagara River into Canada. I didn't catch all the words, but thinking they must have been shouting something unfriendly, I flipped them the bird. My wife looked at me inquisitively and asked me why I did that. They had yelled, "Welcome to Canada!" Paranoia knows no limits.

Racial discrimination is not much different from caste discrimination. In India, I witnessed caste discrimination on an almost daily basis. It was evident in contrast between the sacrilegious ways servants and people doing menial jobs were treated and the reverence offered to priests and anyone who wore a tie or spoke a few English words. Nowhere is the inhumanity of India's caste system more evident than in the social ostracization of the Dalits, the so-called "Untouchables."

Several years ago, my family built a temple in Jodhpur, Rajasthan, in honor of my godmother, Dahimasi, and my mother. It is built on the grounds of a residential school for physically handicapped children. Our charity, *Polio Children*, had been supporting the school for almost fifteen years. We had become aware of severe emotional problems these children face as a result of and in addition to their physical challenges. A quiet place where they could pray, meditate, and regroup would help them heal.

At the ceremony to consecrate the temple, I noticed Rajoo, our driver, standing outside the temple. I motioned him to enter but he didn't move. He turned his gaze down. Later, he revealed that his family was of the Dalit caste. As a member of the lowest Indian caste, he knew he was not allowed to enter "our" temple.

I grabbed his arm and pulled him into the temple. He was clearly uncomfortable. The memory from that incident that has stayed with me is that of his sad affect. It mirrored my own feelings.

Whatever historical merits of the caste system there may have been, it serves little purpose today. However, the customs, rites, and practices based on it are so pervasive and deeply ingrained that only a social tsunami may rectify the state of affairs it has created.

The joy of giving

My primary interest in medicine was parasitology. It was probably piqued by several childhood events. Once I watched in fascination as our house servant Petro used a matchstick to wind up and remove a guinea worm from a child's leg. The child's relief from agony was almost immediate. As children, when we went digging for earthworms for bait, my friends would scoop them up with a large lump of clod, but I would tease them out and study them closely on my palm. In medical school, I had been deeply intrigued by the subject. My interest was further reinforced by an excellent teacher.

But when I explored training options in parasitology in the UK, I was told there were few. Psychiatry residency was relatively easy to get into. I thought I would spend a year in psychiatry, get some experience under my belt, impress a couple of consultants who would give me glowing references, and then resume my hunt. But a bird in the hand is worth two in the bush. And I enjoyed visiting patients in their homes and evaluating their mental health needs within their own environments and not in a hospital bed. So I joined a four-year psychiatric training program that would take me through various hospitals in North Yorkshire, starting with Scarborough.

In the first week of my training, I came across an advertisement from Save the Children Fund in the local paper. The charity was founded in the UK in the early twentieth century to improve the lives of children around the world through educational, health care, and economic support. It was the first global movement for children that advocated for their rights. For a few pennies a day, the advertisement said, a child's life could be turned around. Accompanying the advertisement was a black and white photo of a young, emaciated Filipino girl dressed in a frock looking forlornly at the camera. *Really?* I thought. *Less than the cost of a pint of British brew would give this child a life that she would otherwise not live just because she happened to be born in a poor family?*

The memories of my time on the pediatric unit in Zambia and the unrelenting morbidity and mortality of the African babies came flooding back to my mind.

When I was in Zambia, I wanted to ease the children's suffering but did not have the resources to do so. My small stipend barely covered my living expenses. I could have siphoned away a few *kwachas* from my beer budget, but I didn't. Now, a real opportunity presented itself.

I tore out the advertisement from the newspaper and started filling it out. For some reason, the pledge required the signature of a witness. I grabbed Sister Rawling who was passing by. She was pleased to oblige. I took an early lunch, walked to the post-office, and dropped off the envelope.

A few weeks after I sent in my first donation to the Save the Children Fund, I received a letter from a field director in the Philippines. The letter was accompanied by a black and white photograph of a beautiful Filipino schoolgirl. Unlike the photo in the advertisement, this girl looked healthier and she had a puckered smile on her face. I tried to make a connection with her. "Don't worry. You will go places," I told the girl in the photo.

I did not know it then, but something deep within me had been kindled.

Superior Bill

Dr. William Stuart, Bill to his friends, was a burly Yorkshire man who lived on coffee and cigarettes and never touched a morsel of food until dinnertime. Every evening, he would replenish his calories with half a boiled cabbage, meat and potatoes, followed by a dessert of more coffee and cigarettes.

To break the monotony of his cabbage dinners, he would occasionally suggest we eat out. The invitations were like god-sent gifts for me. My aptitude for cooking was in the zero-range, but I was a foodie. Bill would almost always opt for an Indian restaurant. Over time, I came to know why.

He held a deep affection for many things Indian. He knew his spices and the subtle flavors they added to cooked dishes, what chili star-rating to order so that you did not leave your tongue behind in the restaurant, and what beers went best with spicy dishes.

As alcohol started circulating in our veins, my tongue loosened, as did his stiff upper lip. He was a good conversationalist. Our banter would shift from psychiatry to the more interesting topics of culture, society and more—issues sober people hold close to their chests.

Once when both of us were well-lubricated, Bill asked me about the strange, tong-like steel tool he had seen amongst my toiletries in our communal bathroom. I briefly described the function of the tongue cleaner, hoping to move on to less putrid topics.

But he continued: "Why do you have to put on an apologetic tone when you are explaining your Hindu customs and habits?"

I immediately became defensive and said something like, "Apologetic? Nah! It's just your British sense of superiority complex."

But Bill would have the last word.

"No need to feel inferior," he retorted.

Perhaps there was a kernel of truth in Bill's assessment.

Collegial consultants

After completing my first year of psychiatric training in Scarborough, I moved forty miles south-west to York. The beautiful walled city is famous for its cathedral, the York Minster, and its narrow, cobbled streets like The Shambles.

In our training program, we were blessed with thoughtful consultants. It hadn't been that long ago that they themselves had been through the rigors of night calls and the stress of writing exams. They did what they could to ease some of our travails.

All-day events a consultant couple hosted from time to time provided memorable stressbusters. All the trainee doctors and consultants would meet at the couple's lovely cottage just outside York. Dr. Bromham, ever the gracious host, would lay out a huge brunch. All kinds of dishes waited for us, and her husband made sure the drinks flowed freely. Soon there would be good-natured bantering—we needed their references, after all—between the junior and senior doctors. We would forget our looming exams, if just for the day.

Late in the afternoon, all of us half-inebriated, a cricket match would start. Only the consultants were allowed to hit the ball out of the small ground. A junior trainee would have to retrieve it. Seniority has its perks.

As the evening rolled in, we moved indoors for more drinks and food. It would be pitch black by the time we would leave our friendly hosts' home. Everyone would get home safely, eventually.

An academic setback

With a clang, the mail slot cover snapped to a close. At its sound, I ran to the front door.

I had managed to sleep only fitfully that night. My exam results were due in the mail the following morning. After dawn, I awoke several times with a start, thinking I had heard the mailman. This time, it was for real.

My heart pounded as I slit open the envelope.

Disaster! I had failed the first part of the post-graduate psychiatric exams.

I called Nitin to find out how he had fared. He had passed.

After our mini detours to Africa, Nitin and I had both joined psychiatric training programs. As fate would have it, the hospitals we were attached to were both in the county of Yorkshire. He was in Doncaster in the west and I was far north in Scarborough. We visited each other frequently, even rearranging our schedules to watch the FA Cup Final together. Fueled by curried chicken and beers, we remained glued to the television for several hours watching the nation's biggest sporting event—the English equivalent of Super Bowl Sunday.

I took my failure very hard. I felt depressed, worthless, and helpless —a failure in more ways than one. It consumed me to the point that I could think of nothing else.

My mind would go through each section of the exam that I had failed. For hours on end, I would play the rumination game of "What if?" What if I had chosen to answer question number two instead of number one? What if I had skipped answering rather than hazarding guesses for the multiple-choice questions on neuroanatomy? Then I might have accumulated fewer negative marks

My non-stop introspection took its toll. I felt utterly desolated, I had difficulty concentrating at work, and I withdrew socially. I became convinced my British colleagues were thinking, "Dr. Patel. Poor guy can't get through Part 1. It really is tough for these foreign doctors." So, I started avoiding them.

In tandem with my post-graduate psychiatric qualification, I had been pursuing a Master of Medical Sciences degree. I quit the course midway, despite being one of the few to have passed the first part, so low was my self-confidence. Now I wish I had not. I was halfway there. If I had had the benefit of the sage advice of my future boss, Dr. Paul Tufts, "If you want to commit suicide, wait until *mañana*. Things will be different," perhaps the outcome would have been different.

During my self-imposed time in the penalty box, I grasped at any straw I could clutch. Arun found a seer who recommended wearing a green stone on a gold ring and fasting on Thursdays. A wristband of red and orange colors would fend off the evil spirits or hopefully mellow the examiners. I followed these recommendations half-heartedly. I had neither the conviction nor the commitment to give them a good run.

A forced sabbatical and a wedding

After I failed again in my third attempt to pass the psychiatric exam, I had to sit out for a year. The logic behind the year out was that it would give the candidate time to prepare better. I did not feel I needed more time. I needed better luck!

Something good, though, came out of my forced sabbatical.

Shashi and I decided to tie the knot. The civil ceremony took place on a beautiful sunny day in October 1986. Later that evening, a few of us went to a local pub for a stag night. Then it was back to work for two weeks before the traditional Indian wedding in Leicester, Shashi's hometown. A week's honeymoon in alpine Austria, and it was again back to work and preparations for more exams.

Shashi had qualified as a pharmacist in England and had been working for a couple of years when we first met. She quickly found a job in York after our marriage. While all her evenings and weekends were free, I was either on-call or studying for one exam or another. After a few months of observing my routine, she decided to join me. She would study for the US pharmacy exams.

Having company in studying was helpful. But I could not wait for the day when the exam, work, exam cycle would end. My feelings of anger and frustration would spill out now and again. Shashi tells me these instances amused her more than they baffled her.

Back on track

Ultimately, Nitin came to my rescue. Conscious that he had succeeded where I had failed, he was initially hesitant to give me unsolicited advice. But after I failed to get through the exam three times in a row, he let me have it.

"You probably don't realize this, Shirish, but you became quite cocky after you passed the first part of the Master of Medical Sciences exams. And you had the audacity to go on a vacation just before the last exam," he told me. "What's more, your exam preparations have had a very narrow focus. These are not undergrad exams. You have to be prepared for the most unexpected questions," he continued.

I felt broadsided. But Nitin was not done. He went on to systematically review my performance in each of the exams and point out my strengths and weaknesses. Finally, he shared with me the plan he had used to study for the same exams, in case I was interested.

The penny had dropped, and I regrouped.

In quick succession, I managed to pass both parts of the psychiatric exam. During the oral section of the exams, one of the examiners noted, "You are answering so well that we are running out of questions!" Most candidates would have interpreted the remark as a sure sign of passing the exam. But my past failures had made me so pessimistic and had eroded my confidence to such a low level that I still worried whether or not I had done enough to pass. Failure has a way of twisting one's psyche.

Just before obtaining the coveted Membership of the Royal College of Psychiatrists, I had cleared the exams for international medical graduates that allow them to apply for a training position in the US. I mailed out more than six hundred applications to all the lower 48 states, and I managed to get three interviews.

In November 1988, Shashi and I landed in Rochester, New York. I would be pursuing a fellowship in geriatric psychopharmacology at the University of Rochester. It was a dream come true to work on two of my favorite subjects—pharmacology and Alzheimer's disease. After what felt like a long period of derailment, my career was back on track.

Nitin and his wife Reeta had moved to Baltimore, Maryland, six months earlier.

When it rains, it pours.

Five:
Lessons in Loss, Life, & Leadership in the USA
1988-2020

I resolve to be mindful of my speech. I will use my words to heal and not hurt. I will try to listen carefully and act responsibly.

—from Swami Tyagananda's
Walking the Walk: A Karma Yoga Manual

Losses

P lease tell my brother that I wish him a happy birthday," I told the nurse at the other end of the line before hanging up.

My younger brother Nanu had been hospitalized in London a few days earlier. When I called his ward, the nurse told me that he was not in a state to answer the phone. My family had told me that this time around, he seemed much worse than before. He passed away the following day, a day after his 40th birthday.

Nanu had had a rough life with frequent illnesses and multiple surgeries. When he was 24 years old, a rare large intestine bleeding condition required a permanent colostomy. On many occasions, I witnessed him struggle to change the colostomy bags. His frail and failing state did not make it easy for him. During my medical career, I had seen many patients with a colostomy, but none that I could remember experienced as much difficulty with it as Nanu.

I had mixed feelings about his passing away.

Nanu had gradually wasted away over the previous ten years as his body failed to assimilate any energy and seemed to be feeding on itself. A few years before his demise, we went shopping for a pair of trousers for him. The extent of his weight loss became evident when we had to go to the children's section because his waist had shrunk so much. He was in constant pain. My medically trained mind could see the very poor quality of his life.

But he was my brother. My younger brother. How could one think ill about one's own flesh and blood?

As with my father's death, my initial reaction was one of feeling devastated. Although there was a gap of fifteen years between their deaths, I doubt age makes accepting personal losses any easier. For me, though, reflecting on his life and trying to understand his death in the context of what I had learnt spiritually definitely helped.

Nanu's health problems began at a very young age. He had undergone major surgeries and prolonged hospitalizations. But never once did I know him to lose hope. Whenever he could, he enjoyed the small pleasures of life to the fullest. Mostly, these would be in the form of ham sandwiches sold on the British Rail and watching his beloved English cricket team trounce the Indians, much to our chagrin.

Nanu was not a religious person. But as was his style, he would sometimes surprise us with his questions and thoughts. This did not occur very often, but when it did, he would leave us all intrigued.

One day, he asked my older sister, Shobhi, "Have you been on the other side?"

Confused, Shobhi asked, "What do you mean by 'the other side'?"

He gestured to the heavens. Without waiting for her response, he smiled and said he had.

I am sure I am not the only one to ponder and agonize over the unwelcome and dreaded events of disease and death in the circle of life. At an intellectual level, I can accept them as inevitable events. But at an emotional level, accepting them is difficult. However, viewing them spiritually makes morbidity and mortality meaningful and acceptable. A spiritual perspective provides comfort and lessens the pain.

I believe it all boils down to karma. There is no need for me to judge or blame anyone. We are all creators of our own destinies.

> *Even as we cast off worn-out garments*
> *And put on new ones, so casts off the Self*
> *A worn out body and enters into*
> *Another that is new.*
>
> —*The Bhagavad Gita*, trans. by Eknath Easwaran

In Rochester, I was privileged to work under Dr. Paul Tufts, who would go on to become an internationally recognized researcher in Alzheimer's disease. In his Laboratory of Psychopharmacology, we tried to understand the chemical mechanisms underlying memory problems and to explore possible treatment options.

One mechanistic approach involved studying memory functions in patients with Parkinson's disease. The illness mostly affects elderly people and manifests itself with shakes and difficulties with walking and balance. In the later part of the illness, many develop problems with their mental faculties.

Paul and I would go to senior citizen centers and Parkinson's disease support groups to recruit participants for the study. Since each study day was almost a half-day long, there was plenty of idle time to chit chat with the participants. Most of them had funny tales to share. But one gentleman seemed angry all the time and said little. Thinking he was unhappy with some aspect of the study, I asked him what had made him sign on. After all, participation was voluntary and we did not offer any financial compensation. He told me his story.

One of his passions was reciting works of William Shakespeare. He and a friend of his, an even greater fan of the Bard of Avon, had planned to walk the coast of England while reciting the great poet's works. Several years had gone into formulating the plans. He even had a ramp installed at his home so that whenever his wife decided to use a wheelchair when he was gone, she could do so with ease. All systems were *go* when a few months before he was due to retire and embark on his trip, he was diagnosed with Parkinson's disease. His lifelong dream was squashed.

I could understand his bitterness.

At about the same time, I learnt that my college roommate, Harry, had passed away. We had lost contact after college when he left for further studies in Australia. I had heard that he had developed a brain tumor but was doing well back home with his family in Zimbabwe.

A beautiful, bubbly spirit had been extinguished in its prime.

A priceless gift

"Please God, help Shashi carry this one to term," was my instant silent prayer when I saw *Normal... 22 XX* on the amniocentesis report that lay on the fax machine. A healthy baby girl! Perhaps we would be fourth-time lucky.

Almost 30 years before when I had found out that my mother was pregnant with my younger sister, Meeta, I had been so ashamed of it that I had vowed never to have any children of my own. Mercifully, paternal yearnings had eclipsed the sophomoric promises I had made to myself.

To our boundless joy, our daughter was born on the last day of the month of March. A day later and people would have thought her forty-year-old parents were in April fool's mood!

Entering civil service

In 1994, after seven years in academics and research, I was ready for a change. I would maintain my clinical faculty appointment at the University of Rochester since I thoroughly enjoyed teaching. But my days in the laboratory were coming to an end.

Tentatively, I started a private practice and took a part-time position at the Veterans Affairs Medical Center in Canandaigua, New York. The historic hospital was built in the 1930s on a campus of 120 acres and is located in the beautiful Finger Lakes region of upstate New York.

I found private practice neither gratifying nor challenging. However, in dealing with the garden-variety mental health illnesses of depression and anxiety, I learnt one important lesson. For sustained improvement and recovery from any mental illness, psychotherapy, commonly known as talk therapy, is absolutely essential. Drugs on their own are of limited benefit.

The lesson would prove valuable to me during my sabbatical study several years later.

In 1996, I moved full-time to the veteran's hospital as the Director of Inpatient Psychiatric Services.

Across the country, the Veterans' Health Administration was undergoing tremendous change. America's largest health care system was moving into the twenty-first century at breakneck speed. The transformation was spearheaded by Dr. Kenneth Kizer, Under Secretary for Health in the Department of Veterans Affairs. Under his able and dynamic leadership, new policies were formulated in the nation's capital and disseminated to the 150 medical centers across the country with the singular goal of providing "high quality of care at a lower cost."

At our hospital, orders came to empty out the back wards, where patients had been warehoused for decades. Veterans who had served their country so valiantly deserved to be treated with dignity and respect, no matter how chronic or severe their disabilities. The veterans would be relocated to small group homes in the community and given a chance to lead as normal a civilian life as possible.

The new directives required treating patients using evidence-based treatments. These were driven by scientific evidence, including information obtained from research, experts in the field, and patients, not solely based on healthcare providers' personal experiences. The health care delivery system's historical model built around providers like doctors and psychologists would be dismantled, and the patient would be put in the middle. Evidence-based clinical practice was the new focus and patient-centered care the new locus.

However, change comes faster on paper than in practice.

On our inpatient psychiatric unit, each day began with the nursing staff presenting a report of overnight activities to the multidisciplinary team of providers. Reports of behavioral problems or patient demands generated the most discussion. All kinds of professional opinions were proffered. Rarely did anyone enquire what the patient wanted or what options he had been offered to defuse the situation.

Restricted smoking privileges were the most common cause of disharmony. Smoking was not permitted on the unit and off-unit smoking times were regimented. Tempers frequently flared in nicotine-deprived brains.

When I started asking about patients' preferences, the questions were not well received.

Some of the staff began to adapt to the new policies. But many remained stuck in the anachronistic practices of the 1970s. The latter took my questioning as minimizing their opinions. At one point, a department head asked why I did not return to the ivory tower of academia if I was so unhappy with, as he said, "the way we do things here." But my team and I had invested too much energy promulgating excellent clinical care to be distracted by the naysayers.

In hindsight, I could have done some things differently. I was so engrossed in enhancing patient care and erasing outdated practices that I failed to pay sufficient attention to human factors.

For example, I viewed putting patients into cuff and belt restraints as inhumane. In my effort to minimize, and preferably eliminate, their use, I failed to weigh the nursing staff's concerns for their own safety. I was going by my experience in England. I had never seen, let alone prescribed, this form of restraint. I knew of large inpatient units with similarly disturbed patients that operated without them. But the clientele here was different. More importantly, as the frontline providers, the nurses were not using them injudiciously. They were highly experienced and understandably concerned about their personal safety.

A meeting of minds would have helped immensely. But it never happened.

I have since learnt that most people are not resistant to change. First and foremost, they want to be heard. They want to be acknowledged by someone in authority and know they have been listened to. They want their fears and concerns addressed. They want an opportunity to have a say in matters concerning them and in running a program in which they are integral members.

I have also learnt from personal interactions that most healthcare providers deeply care for their patients. It is just that some of them feel overwhelmed by changes, especially if those changes occur at a fast pace. For others, getting outside their comfort zones is anxiety-provoking.

Appropriate staff training can go a long way to address and alleviate such issues.

Finally, everyone wants to feel reassured that ultimately things will work out if they embrace the changes.

All are perfectly legitimate expectations.

Unforgettable Dr. White

My efforts to promote evidence-based clinical practices met with several obstacles. None was more frustrating than the resistance of certain staff members.

Dr. Helen White was an unforgettable character, and not all for the right reasons. We first met when I joined the veteran's hospital as a part-time psychiatrist. We shared the caseload on a long-term care psychiatric unit for patients with chronic mental health problems such as schizophrenia, post-traumatic stress disorder, Alzheimer's disease, and traumatic head injuries. Many of the patients manifested severe behavioral problems in the form of agitation and aggression. The nursing staff's hands were full, 24/7.

But for the attending psychiatrist on the unit, the work was not that demanding. At least not if one chose the "pill for an ill" approach. That was the approach taken by most of the previous attending psychiatrists on the unit and the approach now favored by Dr. White. Whenever consulted for a behaviorally disturbed patient, her modus operandi was to add another tranquilizer to the patient's already overloaded drug regimen, enter scant documentation to justify the intervention, and allow life on the unit to go on.

As a fellowship-trained geriatric psychiatrist, I had spent the previous four years in an academic and research center studying and treating behavioral problems similar to those we were seeing on our unit. I did not subscribe to the pill-for-an-ill approach. My training had stressed that medications were to be used as a last resort, only after all behavioral interventions had failed. The medications I was trained in were very different from those used traditionally. The latter, antipsychotics and benzodiazepines, have side effects that mimic and may even aggravate behavioral problems—the very symptoms that we are trying to treat in the first place. Professional medical guidelines require that these medications be used judiciously and prescribed by a provider with a certain level of expertise.

I would share my concerns with Dr. White, and she would always listen with a smiling face. But then she would continue her same old prescribing habits.

Her prescribing practices would soon come to cause me a great deal of consternation.

Consummate Sara

In 1997, I was selected to co-lead the department of mental health at the VA Medical Center in Canandaigua. In the lingo of the federal healthcare system, mental health was called *behavioral health*, departments were referred to as *carelines*, and a department leader's title was *careline manager*.

My co-leader was Sara Sheldon, a nurse by profession who had been at the hospital for over ten years when we paired up. She had worked in most of our department's divisions and had firsthand knowledge of what was working and what was not. Sara was not interested in basking in the glamor and perceived power of her new leadership position. She would do whatever it took to rectify the shortcomings of the system we had inherited by putting her remarkable ability to think on her toes to full use.

Sara was a mother of three with strong maternal instincts. When we had to travel to Albany, the state capital, for a meeting, she graciously volunteered to give me a ride. As she picked me up that morning, she asked me to take the back seat. There, waiting for me, was a pillow and blanket. She knew I had just come in on a red-eye flight from the West coast. I slept soundly all four hours of our journey.

Sara and I had full budget and line authority. We had oversight of the six divisions in our careline, including an inpatient unit, outpatient clinics, and a dedicated program for homeless veterans, as well as supervisory authority for over 150 employees. Dr. Kizer's restructuring plan brought all mental health divisions under one roof with singular leadership. The system allowed for seamless care. Patients no longer needed to be shunted from pillar to post.

Our work was immensely aided by the advanced electronic medical records system that the organization had embraced a decade earlier. Patient information was accessible at the press of a button from any location within the hospital. There were no missing blood reports. Or X-rays. Or consultation reports. It was all there on our desktop PC screens.

Veterans Affairs hospitals often get bad press. But if one were to take the time to consider the magnitude of the VA health system, the complexities of its operations, and the tightness of its budget, one cannot help but marvel at its efficiency and the quality of care it provides.

Sara was willing to be patient and work within the constraints of the policies developed in Washington. I, on the other hand, was getting more impatient by the day. I wanted to take the bull by the horns and shake up the entire careline from top to bottom.

Of course, speed is an alien concept in any bureaucratic organization.

"You will cease and desist..."

Fortunately for me, Sara understood and accepted labor relations, of which I knew little. And in my single-minded determination to bring our careline's performance into the top tier, I viewed them more of a hindrance than a help. Not surprisingly, my relations with our local union leaders did not get off to a great start.

I resented that some of them tended to behave like lawyers, though they did not possess any legal credentials. They would throw the book at us at every opportunity—even when our actions were clearly to the benefit of the concerned staff and the patients and detrimental to none. But no! These were the rules. "You will cease and desist," was their favorite refrain.

One time, I urgently had to move a staff psychologist to another unit within our program to take care of emergent clinical needs. The staff member was happy, the losing and receiving unit managers were agreeable to the change, and so were the patients. The bargaining union stewards were not. The mandatory two-week wait had not elapsed since we had submitted the transfer notice. Therefore, the placement would have to wait. So much for the medical center's motto: "Patients First"!

Then there was the time when the outpatient program lead and I were meeting with the union leaders to hash out some kinks related to the implementation of a new clinical process. Midway through our discussions, one of the stewards—who was not a physician—started asserting his opinion of the clinical process. I told him, rather forcefully, that he was not qualified to comment on the clinical attributes of the process and that he should stick to the staffing issues. He made a vague threat about seeing me in court and stormed out of the meeting.

Thus, quite early on in my leadership role, Sara felt that it would be best if she handled our program's bargaining issues and left me out of them altogether. This arrangement suited me just fine because I had a strong suspicion that some of the union stewards carried over the baggage from before.

A year before I assumed co-leadership of the mental health department, I was appointed to a committee by the senior management to address reduction in force. I was president of the medical and dental staff and would be representing their interests. The union steward on the committee maintained that his union represented the doctors and that he would speak for them. I disagreed, and we argued vehemently about it. In the end, I carried the day.

Later, someone pointed out to me in private that the steward was right because of an anomalous arrangement that existed only at our medical center. After the committee's work was done, I bought him a drink at a dinner hosted by senior management. But it seems that did nothing to lubricate our relationship.

Almost a decade later, we would butt heads again. And their client would be none other than the staff psychiatrist with questionable prescribing practices—Dr. White.

Taking the helm

When I was selected to co-lead the mental health careline at the VA Medical Center in Canandaigua, I was also offered a collateral appointment as chief psychiatrist for the Veterans Integrated Service Network 2 (VISN 2). The VISN was one of 23 such networks in the country. Geographically, it extended from Albany in the east to Buffalo in the west, and it comprised five major medical centers and about 30 community outpatient clinics.

Several senior psychiatrists had had their eyes on this coveted position. It was a pleasant surprise when the position was offered to me, but accepting it came with a price. Senior psychiatric leaders passed over were not happy.

Dr. Udas wore his disgruntlement on his sleeve. He had all sorts of tricks to sabotage our monthly meetings and would try to rally other chiefs of psychiatry against me and the new management. He asked questions unrelated to the agenda, for which he had failed to get answers from his own supervisors. He would repeatedly interrupt and ask to move the agenda along, wishing we could finish the scheduled day-and-a-half meeting in a few hours.

I fell back on sage advice. During his annual review of my performance, my Chief of Staff, Dr. Campbell, had said, "You have great potential for leadership in the VA. But learn to pick your battles." So I tried to accommodate some of Dr. Udas's unreasonable demands and put the rest in the parking lot. I knew his demands were mere digressions and a displacement of his feelings of failure. I needed his cooperation to move the agenda along.

Dr. Udas's bruised ego and overt hostility towards the new management did not allow him to see past the end of his nose. When none of his tactics worked and he failed to get any support from the others, he stopped coming to the meetings, instead sending a junior staff member to fill in for him. His destructive behavior prevented us from implementing several evidence-based practices I believe would have greatly benefited our patients. New psychotropic drugs were being introduced into the market at a mind-boggling speed. Creative ideas about multidisciplinary treatment planning and risk assessment for suicide were sprouting all over the place. Many of our bright and eager young psychiatrists were keen to explore new territories. Unfortunately, one individual's selfish motives slowed the group's progress. In debating moot points, we wasted a lot of time and energy.

Futuristic Dr. Mott

If you want to climb up [a corporate ladder], you need a godfather.

—Favorite advice from Dr. James Campbell

During my tenure as a researcher, I was fortunate to have been coached and mentored by Dr. Paul Tufts. Now as I ventured into the leadership arena, I entered Dr. Simon Mott's orbit.

Simon was an articulate, forward-thinking, courageous psychologist who could take it on the chin. He was always smartly dressed and walked with a southpaw gait—his left shoulder a touch higher than the right. He was endowed with excellent leadership qualities and had a keen eye to see the forest for the trees. And he had his funny side, too.

His job was to raise the quality of clinical practice in our network's five medical centers so that the patient care we provided was on par with, or better than, the national standard. He was not one to issue mandates. His style fell more along the lines of healthy debates, concessions and compromises, and maximal involvement of frontline staff. At the end of the day, they were the ones in direct contact with the patients.

His approach was alien to the staff that had worked in a system made of fiefdoms and authoritatively run by chiefs of service, such as psychiatry, psychology, social work, and others. Chiefs zealously guarded their turf. Physicians were used to being heard, not told. In that system, the numerous cogs in the wheel of mental health services kept chugging along, but not in an efficient or effective way. In this archaic model of health care, the services are built around the convenience and comfort of the care providers. The new model would flip things: before all other considerations, patient needs would be of paramount importance.

When Simon assumed the reins, he knew he had his work cut out for him. He rose to the challenge admirably. With a keen eye for human potential, he looked for leaders as hungry as himself to deliver patient-centered mental health care and who were willing to go the extra mile. The management team he assembled consisted of experts in the field and novices, like myself. With his team in place, he steered the ship with a sense of fairness, determination, and perseverance. A few of his new subordinates had been his supervisors in another life. But when he read the riot act to latecomers to a meeting, no one was spared—not even his previous bosses.

Meetings, however, were not kept to a heavy tone. Returning after a break, I would put on my glasses only to find that I could not see well. Upon inspection, I would see that my pair had been swapped with someone else's. Women would find their handbag straps tightly wound to their chairs' backrests. As they struggled to free their purses, Simon would go on conducting the meeting with a straight face. Simon had a genuine people's appeal to him. After chairing an exhausting whole-day meeting, he would buy the first round for all of us.

He knew how to bring out the best in his staff. Once when he was visiting our medical center, the union leaders invited him, Sara and me for pepperoni pizza at lunchtime. Citing my vegetarianism, I tried to get out of the luncheon. Simon just winked at me and said, "Oh! Come on. It's all for brownie points." He was aware my relationship with the bargaining unit folks was at best cold and often outright hostile.

When we returned to my office later that afternoon, I could see he was upset. He told me he was flabbergasted by my behavior. He demonstrated how I had sat in a corner at lunch with my arms tightly wrapped around me, pouting like a teenager denied permission for a night out. He noticed I had hardly uttered a word and had made no effort whatsoever to just shoot the breeze. He wondered aloud why I could not let go of the past and alluded to his perception that there was a lack of mutual respect between the union leaders and me. "You don't have to agree with them, but at least you must acknowledge them if you expect them to listen to you," he concluded.

Simon's astute observation made me realize that union stewards were not the only ones carrying baggage from the past.

Wrangle with EEOC

As Chief of Psychiatry, I maintained a personal interest in the quality of care rendered to our patients. Every quarter, I reviewed several randomly selected charts of the psychiatrists I supervised. During one review, a staff psychiatrist's case threw up a red flag. A huge banner, in fact!

The case belonged to Dr. White, the psychiatrist I had shared responsibilities with on the long term care unit when I first joined the VA in 1994.

As I scrutinized documentation of her care records, areas of serious concern quickly became evident. She had prescribed multiple psychotropic medications simultaneously and failed to take any steps to monitor the safety of the cocktail. Many medications used to treat mental health disorders can have adverse effects on the heart. With concurrent prescription of more than one such medication, the risk multiplies. Safe, prudent clinical practice calls for the use of one psychotropic medication at a time and keeping a close eye on heart health via ECGs.

I consulted with senior management and the human resources department. Pending further review of her cases, Dr. White was placed on administrative leave.

Dr. White's response was to file a complaint with the Equal Employment Opportunity Commission against the organization and name me as the responding management official. Unbeknownst to me at the time, she had resigned from her last job under threat of being fired for clinical inaptitude. Issues related to physician licensing and malpractice are public record. I was shocked to learn that the clinical complaints raised at her last place of employment were almost identical to the problems I had identified. Old habits die hard, I guess.

Thus started a battle that would drag on for nearly seven years.

Dr. White's primary ground for her complaint was race. She varied her descriptions from one deposition to another. After the complaint was dismissed at all the state-level reviews, she appealed to the United States District Court.

The United States Attorney, John Smith, visited me in the clinic to prepare me for my deposition. His very first question to me was, "Do you have a temper?"

I remember feeling acutely despondent. A thousand questions went through my mind. The case was so straight forward. It had been thrown out by the State. What did my temper have to do with anything? Didn't everyone have a temper? And was its expression a crime? Was this trait of mine going to follow me wherever I went? Paradoxically, I could feel myself getting angry. But past depositions had prepared me well, and I did not let my tone or behavior betray my feelings.

I gave him a rhetorical answer: "Well, doesn't everyone have a temper?"

Like a good attorney having verified his information, he saw no need to pursue the point further.

John went on to cite a case in which I had taken our acute inpatient unit psychiatrists, including Dr. White, to task for neglecting the care of a patient. At the time, I felt my anger was justified because they failed to provide basic medical interventions. The patient was reportedly agitated on admission and placed in cuff and belt restraints for the larger part of his four days on the unit. But the attending psychiatrists did not check his bloodwork, perform a baseline ECG, and he was prescribed multiple psychotropic medications. To make matters worse, I only found out about this gentleman from a team member who mentioned his case as an aside.

John asked my opinion about working with women. I knew where he was going with it because gender bias was one of Dr. White's accusations. I calmly told the US attorney that I had never had any qualms about working with or for women or in supervising them. None of my previous supervisors had ever raised any concerns about gender bias on my part. My previous supervisor at the university, Paul, had shared compliments female staff on our team there had paid me. I brought to John's attention that the majority of the program leads I had appointed were females.

He said that a few staff members who had provided depositions supporting Dr. White had expressed their opinion that I treated Indian women better than the rest.

During my 17 years as Chief of Psychiatry, I supervised more than 30 psychiatrists, of whom only one was a woman of Indian descent.

True to his craft, John explored the issue from several different angles. He wondered aloud if my perceived differential treatment of women was part of my culture.

Perhaps taking it too personally, I looked him in the eye and said, "India elected a woman prime minister in the 1960s." That was almost twenty years before a woman ran on a vice-presidential ticket in the USA.

"Well, that's neither here nor there," was his response.

Interesting. He showed little restraint in attributing his perception of my belief to my whole culture but was pathetically slow in acknowledging the accomplishments of my country of origin!

Much to my relief, but not surprisingly, the appeal was dismissed.

From day one, my conscience had been crystal clear. What is sauce for the goose is sauce for the gander. Patient care trumped everything else. But as I found out, the law operates on neither conscience nor intent. Many a time during the lengthy legal proceedings, I felt I was victimized for holding a practitioner to an acceptable standard of care. I often wondered if a Caucasian female were in my shoes, would Dr. White have filed a complaint against her? And what would have been her grounds?

The irony of double standards was not lost on me.

One day I heard a white male leader make a lurid comment about the act he wished a woman to perform on him, his words leaving nothing to the imagination. Shocked, I popped out of my office into the corridor and saw him with two Caucasian female staff, his back to me. I knew both women well. The man was a known bully. I knew that even if I filed a complaint against him, neither of the female staff would come forward and back me up.

Part II
REFLECTIONS

Six:
On Meditation

I resolve to be mindful of my mind. I will try to remain focused on the activity in hand and not allow the mind to be distracted.

—from *Walking the Walk: A Karma Yoga Manual*

Early rumblings

O ne day during my final year of medical studies, I decided to visit the uncle who had arranged my father's immigration to Uganda. Then in his eighties, he was leading a peaceful, almost reclusive life. Though we lived in the same town, I did not see him often. But he was always overjoyed to see me when I visited, and he would insist that we share a meal together before I left. Thus, my plans for a quick, ten-minute visit would stretch into several hours.

On this particular visit, my uncle, who was never known for his subtleties, asked me what I would do with all the money I would be making as a doctor. Without waiting for my response, he launched into a long-winded monologue of the perils and limitations of the material world. The pursuit of material things, he told me, comes at the expense of spiritual needs. He quoted a *sloka* from our scriptures alluding to transcendental reality. For those seeking such reality, he asserted the way was short and swift. All one had to do? Follow simple meditative practices. And unlike many material things, this option was attainable by everyone, irrespective of the person's financial means. Shaking his head with a resigned look on his face, he looked at me and said, "I just cannot understand why one would want to commit spiritual suicide."

I can't say I understood everything he said, or even agreed with him. Who in his right mind would give up the wonderful and entertaining things money could buy? If they did not bring joy and happiness, what possibly could? As a twenty-three-year-old on the cusp of financial liberation and a mint within my reach, I wanted to acquire a lot of toys and enjoy them. The pull of the material world's promised rewards was strong. I figured I would have plenty of time to reflect on my uncle's philosophy when I reached his age.

Fortunately, though, I did not have to wait that long.

The Save the Children Fund's field worker's reports about the Filipino girl I had sponsored during my first year of residency in Scarborough had stirred thoughts about fairness. Why did one child have so little while another was drowning in plenty? Was it just the luck of the draw? Did it boil down to the economic status of the family one was born in? Or was there more to it? Was it selection and deselection by a higher power? Did a higher power actually exist? This last question would inevitably bring my thought cycle to an abrupt stop.

For fear of reprisal, I would quickly mute all thoughts questioning the existence of a Supreme Being. I would imagine the consequences of failing an exam or losing a family member befalling me as a direct result of my blasphemous thoughts. What would start out as an intellectual pursuit would quickly progress to palpable fear. Slamming down the mental brakes, I steered my thinking into less threatening avenues.

At other times, I would wonder if there were more to life than academic success and material comfort. And again I would stifle such thoughts for fear of jinxing my good fortune. I would rationalize that such thoughts were a symptom of greed. That I was expecting too much from life. That I should be grateful for how far I had come at a relatively young age. My father worked all his life but never managed to accumulate a four-figure bank balance. Not to continue to accumulate wealth, I would chastise myself, would be tantamount to a disdainful arrogance. This line of reasoning always soothed my conscience. Reassured, my mind would turn quiescent and I would start enjoying material acquisitions. Yes: I was simply reaping the benefits of my past karma. Such self-delusions have a nicely intoxicating effect on the mind.

However, my conscience would periodically get troubled. It became persistently more so after we moved to Rochester, New York.

In the late '80s, thanks to our Chinese friends, US markets offered a vast collection of toys at an affordable price. Both my wife and I were rapidly moving up our respective professional ladders, and we had the income to show for it. I remember walking in the aisles of a mega-DIY store, checking out the prices of state-of-the-art electric tools. I also remember smiling to myself and secretly reveling in the knowledge that not one of those tools was beyond the reach of my pocket. Graduating from a roll pin punch set to an electric drill was prosperity indeed!

Over the next few years as I continued to indulge in avaricious spending, I began experiencing intense periods of mental conflict. My ruminations came in phases, and they would reach a crescendo, especially when things were going my way. Say I was planning on making a new purchase, such as a car. I would sit for hours on end, pondering the purchase. During my musings, memories of my uncle's view of the material world and my mother's devotional study of Hindu epics would repeatedly intrude into my thoughts. I would feel conflicted, and I would try to suppress the intruding transcendental thoughts with worldly and material thoughts. As the latter better fit my behavior at the time, I would then make a conscious effort to ignore the former.

About this time, my friend Nitin purchased a new luxury car. I immediately started researching the Blue Book and working out my finances in preparation for matching, or even one-upping, my friend. My wife was somewhat surprised because she knew how little interest I had in cars. What happened next is still crystal clear in my mind, some thirty years later.

I remember hearing an inner voice saying, "Really? Nitin is your best friend and all you can think of is one-upping him rather than sharing in his joy?"

It was a painful thought that caused me a great deal of shame. Yet I tried to talk myself out of my compunction. After all, we really needed a new car. What was wrong with getting a deluxe model? It's not like we would be over-stretching our budget.

But I felt disingenuous. So, all my self-talk paved the way for greater introspection. Slowly, very slowly, and with many re-settings to the baseline, my thinking eventually began to unravel.

Spiritual sages

During my annual visits to see my mother in the UK, she would pepper her comments in our discussions and debates about personal challenges in life in quotes from the two most popular epics of ancient India—the *Ramayana* and the *Mahabharata*.

My mother ardently followed the Hindu preachers Moraribapu and Rameshbhai Oza and watched their taped discourses religiously—pun intended. She gave audio cassettes of the same discourses to me. During my commute to and from work, I would listen to them, relegating soft rock played on the local station to weekend entertainment.

These preachers' interpretation of the scriptures resonated with me more than anything I had read. Through modern-day examples in their parables, they brought to life the morals of events that had occurred more than five thousand years ago. In its literal form, the *Mahabharata* is a narration of a war between two sides of a divided family in the arena of *Kurushetra*. Rameshbhai interprets the age-old narrative in the context of the twenty-first century. He explains that the real war we experience is between the selfish and the selfless sides within us, and the arena is our mind. He gives numerous examples to illustrate his point. Many of them resonated with me, especially those relating to the materialistic world. One of my favorites is, "Give and forgive, don't get and forget."

I started accepting that most of my fears were irrational. Over time, I started refuting the notion that there was a deity sitting in heaven, judging my every word and action and dishing out good and bad luck.

Testing times

Just when I was beginning to get comfortable with my new thought process, Shashi miscarried our first child. It was one of the darkest days of our lives. The same day, her brother was killed in an air crash. We were devastated. Shashi's pain was obviously far greater than mine. She suffered unspeakable pain. I had to give her all the support I could. With help from family and friends, we weathered the storm. On that day, a part of me changed forever.

I was tempted to revert to my old beliefs and attribute the tragic events to a Higher Power who was displeased and punishing us for our past misdeeds. But instead, I willed myself to explore my inner self, my *Kurukshetra*, for answers.

If I could not find them, I could at least rest peacefully, knowing I had tried.

Arun the trooper

Arun encouraged me to explore meditation. He had been swept away by Maharishi Mahesh Yogi and his Transcendental Meditation movement. No longer a regular at a pub, Arun avidly read Maharishi's writings and listened to religious discourses for hours on end. This was quite an about-face for a person who rarely set foot in the temple and once hid under his bed to avoid being forced to go.

During innumerable trips to specialty workshops to get custom-fitted calipers for his polio-affected leg, Arun had observed how many of those who worked to fit the braces—not to mention customers—were in wheelchairs. The progressive, paralyzing effects of polio were on full display. I was too naïve to notice, but not Arun. It terrified him. In the 1960s, there were no self-help groups or counselling where he could have received support for his anxiety. You pulled up your socks and got on with it. He made a silent vow that he would do everything in his power to avoid the wheelchair—or at least delay welcoming it into his life as long as he could.

Kanubhai had convinced my father that Arun should pursue a degree in Chartered Accountancy in England. He reasoned that because of Arun's physical handicap, a sedentary job would be most suitable. Moreover, the UK had some of the most handicap-friendly facilities in the world. It was a country that treated its disabled citizens with dignity and respect. At the time, few of our family friends had been to the UK. My father was happy to go along with Kanubhai's advice. Arun validated

Kanubhai's assessment when he qualified as a chartered accountant and set up abode in Her Majesty's land.

Arun had kept himself physically fit right into his mid-40s playing cricket and later golf. But then he started developing weakness in his unaffected lower limb. The condition, post-polio syndrome, can occur anywhere from 10–40 years after the original illness. It has no known cure.

Arun retired his golf clubs, and like everything else he took on in life, he dove head-on into meditation.

I followed Arun's advice. Transcendental Meditation was my first venture into a formal, meditative practice. At the end of the course, my teacher conducted a brief ceremony during which she gave me my *mantram*. Mantram, or its more common variant, *mantra*, is a word or a group of words that has spiritual power and is recited repeatedly, usually in silence.

I practiced silent mantra meditation twice a day for several months but simply could not find the rhythm. My monkey-mind would start wavering a few minutes into the practice or I would fall off to sleep. Although I knew such experiences were not uncommon, especially in novice meditators, I was impatient to "master" Transcendental Meditation. When, not surprisingly, I failed to do so, the physician in me started questioning the efficacy of such an esoteric practice, particularly since the process lacked any laboratory validation.

Sadhguru's teachings

I remained spiritually unfulfilled. I felt increasingly perturbed that something in me was missing, but I could not put a finger on what. Looking for an answer in theory that I had failed to find in practice, I started devouring faith-based and spiritual books. That is how I came across a copy of *Midnights with the Mystic*.

The publication is the result of a series of conversations between a spirituality seeker and Sadhguru Vasudev, founder of the Isha Foundation. In their late-night conversations, Sadhguru interprets ancient yogic sciences for the seeker and shares self-transformation methods with her. The fact that Sadhguru is "a young agnostic turned yogi, a skeptic turned spiritual guide" resonated with me and added appeal to his mysticism. At last, I had landed a practical guide to spiritual practices. To boot, the copy was autographed by Sadhguru himself!

Once again, Arun was there to share his firsthand experiences. Through advanced practice of Transcendental Meditation, he had reached the stage of levitation. One day, so that I could appease my skeptic mind, he graciously allowed me to witness him levitating. With yoga and meditation techniques learnt from courses run by the Isha Foundation, he was able to restore some of the lost power in his lower limbs. "I am living proof that you can successfully put mind over matter," he would say.

Inspired, I enrolled in Isha Foundation's week-long course on Inner Engineering with thirty other spirituality seekers in July 2008. The prescriptive course was delivered by a well-trained disciple of Sadhguru. Taped video recordings of Sadhguru's short but intense discourses were presented at regular intervals throughout the week. All were riveting. Facts of life, the everyday struggles of the human mind, and simple solutions to end those struggles were forcefully, yet eloquently, delivered. I did not want to blink lest I miss something, so powerful are Sadhguru's choice of words and oratory skills. Add to this his wit, and the week flew by. We were taught *kriyas*, which are a variety of techniques for meditation, breathing exercises, and basic yoga poses. We learnt how to examine our lives, our work, and our world in ways that could lead to our inner peace and spiritual growth.

Back home, I found the daily practice of *kriyas* rejuvenating. Without any effort, I started viewing both my personal and professional lives through a different prism.

My study and implementation of Sadhguru's teachings coincided with the time I was embroiled in Dr. White's EEOC case. Suddenly, preparations concerning the hearing had started moving fast, and I was devoting a considerable amount of time to them. It was my first ever legal wrangle. For several months, I experienced intense anxiety coupled with anger. I was angry because I had never harbored an iota of vindictiveness against Dr. White, and yet I was being made out to be a male chauvinist from India. I had taken it very personally. Through sleepless nights, I played the forthcoming court proceedings in my mind, trying to come up with defensive points that my smart attorney may not have thought of. In hindsight, it is fair to say that the case had consumed me—at least it had to that point.

Practicing *kriyas* added a freshness and clarity to my mind that I hadn't experienced in a very long time. The accompanying physical calm was a welcome relief. Perhaps the most significant change I felt in myself was the almost total absence of fear. I no longer worried about the outcome of the hearing, and I feared it even less. It was as if a cold shower washed away grime that had accumulated on my body during a long walk in the desert.

Several months later, I enrolled in Isha's Hatha Yoga residential course at their beautiful mountain retreat in McMinnville, Tennessee. Over two days, we learnt almost eighty *asanas*, yoga poses. I became reacquainted with the muscles I had last seen in a cadaver in anatomy class at medical school.

Allowing my chronically bad back wide latitude, I incorporated selected *asanas* into my pre-kriya morning routine. Over time, I was thrilled that I could touch my toes without bending my knees. But all good things in life come to an end.

One day I bent down to perform *Surya Namaskar*, the Sun Salutation, when severe pain in my back radiated down my right thigh. For a minute or so, I was completely immobilized. With great difficulty, I sat down only to find my pain level shooting up. I lay flat on the floor but could not find a comfortable position. This was not normal back pain.

An MRI scan would reveal two prolapsed intervertebral discs, one of which was fractured.

Murphy's law was probably in play, but I never was able to dissociate the cause from the effect.

My spiritual guru: Sri Eknath Easwaran

About two weeks into my recovery from the broken back, my wife decided that my fifteen-out-of-ten pain score had come down to a single digit. Locking away my narcotic painkillers, she empathized: "It will clear your foggy mind... and your bowels." Her action was fortuitous. I arrived at the feet of my guru.

While my pain had abated significantly, my mobility was severely limited. I worked remotely from home. Sara, my co-manager, had assumed the bulk of my responsibilities in collaboration with another physician. At home, left with hours to kill, I buried myself into one of my favorite passions, reading.

The Hindu scriptures consist of 30 books organized into six volumes in historical order. After the Vedas, the most ancient and revered of the texts, come the fourteen main Upanishads. These soul-stirring treatises are followed by the *Bhagavad Gita*, considered the holiest by most Hindus, the *Ramyana*, the *Mahabharata*, and the *Dhramasastra*.

After listening to the religious discourses of Moraribapu and Rameshbahi Oza, I wanted to find out what it really meant to be a Hindu. How should I lead my life? I had long detached myself from most ritualistic practices of my religion. I wanted to move beyond the rehearsed dictates of "Hindus don't eat meat. Cows are sacred animals. Respect your elders." These beliefs had been grounded into my DNA over five decades. I was no longer content to lead a passive life. I wanted to take the reins of my life in my own hands and travel down the path of spirituality that would help me find answers to my broodings. I needed a guiding light.

I searched high and low for a book that would give me the answers, like looking for a review article on a disease that summarizes everything —lock, stock, and barrel—known about that subject to date. I found several titles and read and tried to digest them. Unfortunately, none met my needs. The Sanskrit *slokas* were nicely translated into English but the brief commentaries by the author that followed still left me at sea.

Through serendipity, destiny, or karma, my search led me to Sri Eknath Easwaran's *Essence of the Upanishads*. It is the most life-changing book I have ever read. And this is no cliche.

Sri Eknath (*Sri* is an honorific title) was born in India and came to the United States in 1959. At the University of Berkeley, California, he conducted one of the first courses on meditation ever held at a major university. The course was well-received, and two years later, he founded the Blue Mountain Center of Meditation in northern California.

Before coming to the States, Sri Eknath was an English department chair at a university in India. His mastery of the language comes through in every sentence of his writing. Teaching was close to his heart. My academic mind found these two attributes, coupled with his tremendous wit, appealing. What appealed to me even more was that his teachings were based on his personal practices and experiences which were deeply grounded in the scriptures of all religions. Not just Hinduism's *Bhagavad Gita*, but also Buddhism's *Dhammapada*, Christianity's Holy Scriptures, and Islam's *Qur'an*, amongst others. He had read and interpreted those scriptures, making them meaningful to a twenty-first century seeker. In doing so, he left the original scriptural text intact should the reader chose to interpret it differently.

Unlike the other interpretations of the Hindu scriptures that I had read, Sri Eknath opens his version of the Katha Upanishad by naming the hero of the "story." Scriptures narrated in a story form? How brilliant! It reminded me of the gripping writings of Dominique

Lapierre in which historical events are viewed through the eyes of a few key players in the arena.

Sri Eknath deftly collects the pearls of wisdom scattered over the spiritual landscape, arranges them in a logical and coherent sequence, and creates a beautiful necklace that garlands the question, "Who am I?", each pearl offering a simple but deep insight.

6.1 – Sri Eknath Easwaran

He clarifies the role of karma beautifully. *Karma* is defined as something we do, an action. The source of karma are our thoughts. From our thoughts flow words and actions. Every action has its own consequences. Therefore, we reap what we sow.

His interpretation of karma appealed to me for several reasons. The buck started with me and stopped with me. No outside agency, natural or supernatural, bestowed karmas on me. My fate was not predetermined. It was determined by my thoughts, words and actions. I had a choice. While I could not change the path of my current existence because I was reaping or paying for the karmas of my last life, I *could* impact the quality of my future life by leading my present life in a karmic way.

I was also attracted to Sri Eknath's teachings because he was a devoted follower of Mahatma Gandhi. I had idolized the Great Soul since my childhood and later would come to adopt one of his famous sayings to guide me: "To find yourself, lose yourself in the service of others."

I would return to *Essence of the Upanishads* many times over the years, but the most important message I took away from my first reading was that all answers to my spiritual questions resided within me. If I could accept this premise unequivocally and with all my heart, I could bring about changes in my life. I did not have to rely on an external entity. When this message finally sunk in, I felt utterly liberated.

At last, I had discovered a roadmap that appealed to me. It would help me pursue my journey of spiritual discovery and growth. All I needed was the right vehicle. Sri Eknath provided that, too, in the form of Passage Meditation.

On a firm footing

As children, my mother had taught us to recite Rama's name whenever we were in any kind of difficulty. I would do so if I was sick or afraid.

Once, I was down with malaria. The bone-breaking pain was unbearable, and painkillers worked for only short spurts. I started repeating the Lord's name quietly. As my body drowned in sweat, I continued repeating: *Rama, Rama, Rama.* It helped. I don't know whether repeating the mantram helped distract my mind away from the pain or whether it calmed me down sufficiently to put me to sleep. But I remember it helped.

Decades later, I revisited the experience of the calming practice of repeating a mantram, albeit under the auspices of a structured program. There are basically two ways of mastering the thinking process: one is meditation, the other is repeating a mantram. I had tried repeating a mantram as a standalone exercise when I had practiced Transcendental

Meditation, but, as noted earlier, without success. I was hoping meditating on the words of a passage would yield better results.

The system of meditation developed by Sri Eknath is an eight-part process. Called *Passage Meditation*, it evolved from the lessons he had learnt through decades of personal practice. The first part involves meditating on a passage. With proper and regular practice, it takes a person beyond the limits of his or her conscious mind. I had theoretical knowledge about the realms of the mind and wanted to visit them.

I started with memorizing the Prayer of St. Francis of Assisi. Over the next several weeks, I memorized a few inspirational passages from the Bhagavad Gita, the Dhammapada, and the Upanishads. To ensure my practice did not get mechanical, I added to my repertoire a variety of shorter passages including Lao Tzu's "The Best," Fakhraddin Ar-Razi's "Remember Me Through Grace," and the Prayer of St. Teresa of Avila. Once adequately equipped, I poured myself wholeheartedly into the practice of Passage Meditation. I have not looked back, or sideways, since.

Every morning, after completing my self-care activities, I head to the basement in my house where I have carved out a niche specifically for meditation. I sit on a low yoga stool on the floor, tuck my legs under the seat, and gently close my eyes. Then I start performing *pranayama*, the yogic practice of breathing alternately from each nostril while clasping the other one shut with either the thumb or the pinky. After about five minutes, I put my hands in my lap and switch to chanting the auspicious word, *aum*, considered to be the primordial sound of universal creation. I learnt both of these practices during Sadhguru's Inner Engineering workshop a few years before and found that they created a fitting platform for me to segue into Passage Meditation.

I always start my meditation with the Prayer of St. Francis of Assisi and continue on, uninterrupted, to one of the longer passages I have memorized. At the end of thirty minutes, I gently open my eyes and sit for a minute or so, relishing the peace that has descended upon me.

The technique is to allow each word of the passage to enter one's consciousness gently and slowly while concentrating on its sound and meaning: *gently*, like "pearls falling into a clear pond," and *slowly*, so that the words are neither cramped together nor too far spaced out to allow extraneous thoughts to intrude. Each preceding and following word are connected to the central word like the stakes of a picket fence.

Within a short time of performing Passage Meditation, I noticed two novel aspects of this practice deeply resonated with me.

First, the practice held my attention and concentration. And if they strayed, the words of the passage I was reciting would bring them back to the fold. Once again, Sri Eknath uses an apt analogy to explain how reciting a passage can pacify the monkey mind. He compares the human mind to that of the trunk of a domesticated elephant making its way through a row of fruit and vegetable stalls in a bazaar. The pachyderm moves its trunk in all directions, searching for any fruit or vegetable it can land to gulp down. To prevent this theft, the *mahout* gives his pet a bamboo shaft to carry in its trunk. Thus occupied, the elephant passes through the bazaar without pinching any produce. Reciting the words of a passage is akin to carrying a bamboo shaft. The recitation keeps the mind occupied and focused, preventing its distraction.

Second, unlike during mantram meditation, I have never dozed off while meditating on passages. For me, repeating the same word over and over moves the meditation process into autopilot and allows my mind to wander off to bed, whereas with passage recitation, the words constantly change, requiring sustained attention and concentration.

After a few months of practice, I gradually started incorporating the other seven elements of the program into my daily life. Of these, I have been most consistent with spiritual reading and, in keeping with my introverted nature, least consistent with joining others in spiritual fellowship. I try repeating a mantram whenever I remember to do so. Honestly, though, it happens only when I am under stress. But slowing down, one-pointed attention, and putting others first have manifested and increased in strength with practice and time. Training my senses, especially when it comes to resisting goodies, has been the most challenging.

My narrative of meditative practice would be incomplete if I did not mention a couple of experiences. The descriptions may come across as inadequate, which is what happens when one attempts to put spiritual experiences into words.

Sometimes within a few minutes of starting to recite a passage, I feel waves emanating from my body. The feeling is not unpleasant at all, and it comes and goes. However, almost invariably at the end of a session during which I have had this experience, I get a profound feeling of peace and quiet. It is as if, for a minute or so, my mind has become completely devoid of all thoughts. I like to think that the waves represent spiritual transcendences. But the experience itself is more important than its interpretation.

The other experience is "seeing" myself standing outside my physical self and observing my body meditating. The image is not in high-pixel resolution; it is more of an impression that comes and goes. The mental health term used for such an experience is *depersonalization*, and it is often triggered by severe stress. I find it interesting that I experience it when I am relaxed—well at the other end of the stress spectrum.

Peeling off layers

Om Swami gave up his wealth as a young man to become a monk and spread spirituality. In his seminal book, *Kundalini—An Untold Story*, he writes that to reach our innermost state of bliss and joy we must first shed the ten layers—anger, desire, greed, attachment, ego, passion, jealousy, hatred, fear, and self-concern—covering it.

By the time I read his book, I had been meditating for several years. I had accepted that achieving bliss was too far-fetched a goal for me. But I was pursuing each day determined to make every moment as joyous as possible. Of course, fifty years of old habits do not disappear overnight, nor does reading a handful of books bring about immediate results. Yet, Om Swami's message gave me a pleasant jolt. Through my self-study of

Sri Eknath's writings, I had started focusing on three unsettling key areas of my life.

Taming anger

My parents, siblings, and some of my friends had at various times commented on my irascibility. I did not always accept their opinions. Sometimes I found what I thought were plausible explanations for my behaviors. At other times, I thought my actions were simply funny— like the time I angrily threw a golf club after an errant shot. The club got caught on a tree limb and it took some time to retrieve it. In the clubhouse afterwards, my playing partners recounted the incident with amusement. But they were quick to point out that more often than not they found my aggressive behavior on the course distracting.

Gradually, I came to accept that my antics were not normal. Once I accepted that I had temper issues, I made myself accept that anger had no value. Nada, nil, zip. Spiritual readings convinced me: there was no middle ground. That validation encouraged me to do something about my anger. If it could not be extinguished altogether, then at least the self-destructive emotion had to be buried. The combination of my awareness of my churlish behavior and my acceptance of it made it easier for me to initiate corrective action.

I knew I was somewhat hypersensitive, which made me take some comments and disagreements personally. The sage words of a colleague came back to me: "Leaders are supposed to have broad shoulders." I began making a conscious effort to listen to my inner voice and to pay attention to my physical state of being. I paid particular attention to these when I sensed an argument developing or someone contradicting me.

As the chief of service at work, many issues landed on my desk for final resolution. Making executive decisions was not that difficult given that ours was a bureaucratic system guided by a zillion written policies.

Once a nurse program manager under my supervision came to my office waving a sheaf of papers. She was highly agitated and demanded to know how I expected her to run her program when I had approved leave for several doctors to all be off at the same time. Before coming to my office, she had let the doctors know she was going to ask me to cancel their leaves. The doctors had pre-emptively called, upset since they had already made plans and it was too late to cancel. In no uncertain terms, they voiced their resentment at what they perceived as a non-physician treading on their sacrosanct territory.

I listened to the program manager patiently, reminding myself that she was not challenging me personally nor questioning my authority. When she had run out of steam, I explained my rationale for granting the leaves. One was a scheduled leave, another a family emergency, and the third was writing his exams. Also, I let her know I would be available as a back-up, if needed.

A few minutes after she left my office, one of the doctors called me. He said, "What did you tell Jane? She is all smiles and wants to meet with us to work out coverage!"

I reflected on the incident. How many times had I previously cut off a person without listening to his or her full story? How many times had I pulled rank to overrule a subordinate? Same type of scenario, a very different approach, with the same result. But this time, no mental calories had been wasted.

I continued to heed my inner voice. I started loosening the reins and lending the staff my ear. I became aware that as anger started to rise in me, my breathing would pick up pace and become shallower, and I would start shaking my head rather vigorously. I forced myself to stifle both reactions by focusing on my breathing and regulating it down.

I am not sure what effect the change in my behavior had on the staff, but I felt lighter and less tired at the end of the day. It did not take me long to realize that first and foremost, people want to be heard. For most, successful resolution of concerns is a secondary issue. Anger on either side is just a hindrance. I could not control other people's emotions, but I certainly could mine.

Interestingly, as I paid attention to my own ire, I started noticing early signs of anger in others, in the tones of their voices, in their body language, and in their behaviors. This awareness arose not just at work but also in social gatherings and in public places.

Fears released

When I was growing up, I had an intense fear of darkness. On its own, darkness did not pose much of a problem. But when my vivid imagination populated it with images of thieves and ghosts, scenes of murders, and thoughts of other life-depriving elements to the mix, darkness became an unpleasant companion.

Some of my fears were rational. As a child, I had witnessed thieves beaten to death for a crime as petty as stealing a woman's handbag. Local newspapers were filled with reports of housebreakings and attacks on occupants. Of course, our family home had also been broken into— and more than once. Only my father's sharp hearing had saved us. In one village, a family friend hid in his outdoor toilet with his wife and infant daughter while robbers ransacked his shop and his home for hours. A neighbor who challenged robbers who had broken into his home was severely beaten, and he carried physical and psychological scars for the rest of his life. These murderous and near-mortal events put a blemish on the last few years of my time in Uganda.

Otherwise, we had enjoyed ourselves with joyful, carefree spirits in that land blessed with its beautiful climate and truly friendly people. Ask any Ugandan Asian and he will reminisce about his time there with such deep nostalgia that you would think that he had left his country only recently, not almost fifty years ago. No *mwana nchi*—son of the country—will ever forget the sweet memories of his homeland.

After moving to India and later to England, both countries with better law and order conditions, my fear of robbers abated. However, the seat vacated by robbers was taken over by another mortal terror.

In medical school, I had encountered death in multifarious ways. During my first clinical rotation, an elderly gentleman dropped dead right in front of my eyes, just as I was getting ready to interview him. A child bitten by a rabid dog breathed his last as our attending waved a glass of water in front of him to demonstrate the rarely seen symptom of hydrophobia—fear of water. And then there was the case of a dowry death from self-immolation that had a long-lingering effect on all who witnessed it.

Putlibai was a beautiful twenty-three-year-old woman with large brown eyes and long silky hair. Even before she was wheeled into the examining room, we caught a whiff of her burnt flesh. She lay on a trolley wearing only charred *ghaghri-kabjo*, the traditional undergarments of a long skirt and a blouse worn by most Indian women. She was delirious from the burns that covered 90% of her body. As we rushed her to the burns unit, she peeled off the complete skin of her right palm with her left hand as if she was taking off a hand glove. Her action sent shivers up our spines. In witnessing the self-denuding of her palm, it felt to me as if I had witnessed the process of dying. She passed away later that evening.

Death is inextricably intertwined with a doctor's career. As I traversed the landscape of my professional life, it perpetually popped up like the anthills on savannah plains, unsightly and inevitable. Along the way, I adopted various strategies to cope with the cessation of life.

In the early part of residency training, I relied heavily on intellectualizing these terminal events. *You are a doctor. Your job is to treat the patient to the best of your ability. Your job is not to decide who lives and who dies. That is in the hands of the Lord.* This manner of thought worked most of the time as an effective defense mechanism. Moreover, running from one unit to another, admitting new patients, doing blood draws, chasing down X-rays, and the myriad of other clinical duties mercifully left me little time to ponder my feelings.

In the pediatric unit in Zambia, the nursing staff, with their subtle gestures, sympathetic looks, and encouraging words, immensely helped my ability to cope with loss. Yet when weighed down by the inexplicable and meaningless loss of young lives coupled with the sounds of mothers' wailing, my own walls would start to crumble, and I would seek refuge in the doctors' restroom. I would try to make sense of it all. Mercifully, the pager would jolt me out of my gloom. There was no sense to be made.

In the early '80s, there were no programs or formal procedures to help healthcare providers de-stress. To those who sought it, peer support was available. Although as healthcare providers, we did a far better job of comforting the bereaved than tending to our own.

As I progressed through my psychiatric training, I tried various cognitive strategies to insulate my emotions from mortal events. Yes, loss of life is sad. But these are my patients. Not my blood relatives. I cannot take these deaths personally. I must move on. This approach helped me continue to function during the remainder of my residency training and for many years beyond.

It helped, anyway, until I came face to face with the most dreaded part of a psychiatrist's practice. Between 40% to 60% of psychiatrists will lose a patient to suicide in the course of their careers. Regretfully, I am part of that statistic.

John Neesam was a 74-year-old widowed, white gentleman who was referred to me for outpatient follow-up care after his discharge from a local mental health hospital. The discharge summary from the inpatient unit indicated he had been hospitalized against his wishes after he had expressed suicidal thoughts to his girlfriend. The practice of involuntary hospitalization is a common, legal procedure to protect patients with self-injurious tendencies. On discharge, he was deemed to be free of suicidal thoughts, and a plan had been put into place to monitor his safety.

When I saw him in my office, several red flags went up. *Elderly, male, white,* and *widower:* all pointed to high-risk for suicide. My first instinct was to have him readmitted. But he presented hale and hearty, cracked jokes, denied having access to any weapons, and brushed off his recent lethal thoughts as nothing more than fleeting fantasies. His girlfriend, who accompanied him to the visit, endorsed his story and agreed to bring him in for a follow-up visit in a week. He was in a joyous mood and mimicked piggybacking on his girlfriend as they left my office.

Three days later, his girlfriend called me to inform me that after sending her out on an errand, John had shot himself.

I remember feeling shocked. And like many other psychiatrists I have since talked to, the first question I asked myself was, "What did I miss?" I must have dissected his case history to the minutest detail a hundred times. There were no clinical grounds for me to have sent him back to an inpatient unit. His demographics weighed heavily against him, but in themselves, they were not sufficient grounds to admit him involuntarily. It would not have survived a court challenge. Reluctantly, I accepted that if he had managed to fool his girlfriend of three years, I stood little chance of calling his bluff in one hour.

Over time, I have come to accept that an individual who is determined to take his or her life will eventually succeed, no matter what. But that should not stop us from trying to prevent them from doing so. The topic of suicide would rear its ugly face again after I retired when I began teaching in India, and the painful memories of my mother's attempt to take her own life when I was a child would resurface. Due to the way this unsettling topic kept recurring, I vowed to do something about this very preventable human tragedy at the earliest opportunity.

Parting with possessions

Within only a few years of working as qualified practitioners, my wife and I had attained sufficient financial security to start indulging in bling. We bought our first dream SUV, an Isuzu Trooper, and travelled cross-country from Rochester, New York, to Yellowstone National Park. In our new home, we had a top-of-the-line audio/video system with Surround Sound installed, our kitchen remodeled with cherry wood cabinets and state-of-the-art appliances, and several additions constructed to more than double the living area.

Our home became the go-to place for Christmas and New Year's Eve parties. On these occasions, I would clear all the furniture and create a disco floor complete with flashing colored lights and blasting music. Shashi would lay out a huge feast in the adjoining dining room, her multicultural culinary talents on full display. The compliments we received were like music to my ears.

In subsequent years, as I got deeper into spiritual reading and practices, I found myself less enthusiastic about hosting and attending such parties. Meeting with friends to have a few beers and share good food to ring in the New Year still appealed to me. But elaborate preparations and one-upping the previous year's party no longer did.

I was beginning to find comfort in nickel-and-dime purchases—and limiting even those to essentials. This new habit elicited wisecracks from my friends on my two-pence clothing. I laughed them off, sometimes with a crude retort: "But I feel more comfortable when I take them off."

Swami Tyagananda writes in *Walking the Walk*, "A mind filled with desires is a mind that lacks peace and contentment." By detaching myself from material desires, I wanted to create space for spiritual desires and the time for service to the community.

A close friend of mine was once incarcerated for a vehicular mishap. I wanted to send him something tangible to help him in seeing his time through. After a brief period of internal struggle, I sent him an elephant hair bracelet I had received as a present in Uganda in the 1970s. Legend has it that the bracelet brings luck to the wearer, and my friend needed all the luck and support he could get.

Over the years, parting with personal possessions, especially those with sentimental value, has become less and less of a struggle. In one case, my experience was gratifying. The day my daughter turned 21, I gave her a brass key. I had received it 43 years earlier when I had come of age.

As for letting go of amorous as opposed to material desires, the story is different. I take comfort in knowing that more motivated and determined people than myself have not succeeded in curbing them. Whether one views these desires as visceral or carnal, to my mind, the distinction is irrelevant. If they have defied control since time immemorial, what chance do I have?

Having said that, I try to the extent I can and derive strength from Sri Eknath's take on this. He says that if one is able to channel one's libidinal energy into other activities, it is like putting "fuel in a Ferrari."

Now that's a potent incentive!

Seven:
On Religion

Be aware of me always, adore me,
Make every act an offering to me,
And you shall come to me;
This I promise, for you are dear to me.
Leave all other support, and look to me
For protection. I shall purify you
From the sins of the past. Do not grieve.

—*The Bhagavad Gita,* trans. by Eknath Easwaran

Ａs I broadened the scope of my spiritual readings and got deeper into meditation, I started feeling more confident and less fearful of recalibrating my thoughts, beliefs, and practices about religion. During my childhood, my mother's pious teachings laid the foundation for my understanding of Hinduism. Pictures of various deities hung on the walls throughout the house and were placed in the little shrine we had. Except for a few family portraits, these deities were our only wall decor. Many had multiple arms, some of them had several heads, and Lord Ganesh had an elephant head. These images of God, who had many more limbs than an ordinary mortal and possessed supernatural powers, were firmly cemented in my mind. I carried them well into my adulthood.

My mother later introduced Rama, Krishna and other deities with normal human physiques into her parables. These, too, were easy to understand when she explained that they were gods, but they had taken an *avatar*, an assumed earthly form, to protect us, their devotees, from the evil. The pictures confirmed their corporeal likeness to humans, and my mother's parables attested their metaphysical powers.

Ritualistic practices

This paradigm served as the background for the ritualistic practices in our family. We were always eager to participate, not least because most of them were celebrated with delicious dishes specially prepared for the occasion. Spending extra money on indulgences such as chewing gum, soda, and new clothes were additional bonuses. Of these occasions, Diwali, the five-day festival of lights, was the one we most looked forward to.

Several days before the beginning of the festival, my sister, Shobhi, would spend hours creating a *rangoli*. Using brightly colored powders, she designed a beautiful pattern on the floor just inside the main entrance to our house. On the threshold, she drew red swastikas, a symbol of auspiciousness and good fortune in Hindu culture. She would gloat over the compliments our visitors paid.

Each evening, we lit candles in all the rooms in our house. Then after dinner we would all flock outside to The Ground where we spent the next three to four hours lighting fireworks. The young amongst us were limited to wire sparklers while the older ones, under Kanubhai's supervision, put up a show with an assortment of *phatakdas*—bottle rockets, fountains, and whistling wheels.

When I went to India, I was exposed to an even greater number of religious practices than I had been in Uganda. Like the ones I was familiar with, these too were centered around feasting. On some of these occasions, I accompanied my friends to the temple. I would try hard to get involved in the *poojas*, rituals of worshipping and praying to the deities, but I failed to find them appealing or that they satisfied any inner need.

I am not sure I knew what I was looking for or what my inner need was. But I continued to feel unfulfilled. Perhaps a revelation would come to me. Perhaps I would find something more enlightening beyond ritualistic acts of garlanding the deities, offering them food, and singing songs. But no novel experience came my way, so I continued with the daily prayers that I had learnt in my childhood. Mechanically, every morning and evening, I went through the motions. My knowledge base remained stagnant. My search remained unfulfilled.

Paradigm shift

A decade later, the discourses by Moraribapu and Rameshbhai Oza that I listened to during my commute to work helped shift my perception of God from a physical manifestation of a multi-armed, multi-headed superhuman, to an *avatar* whose deeds I needed to emulate. I was not conscious of this shift in my thinking because I was still petrified of being punished for questioning any aspect of God. It would be several more years before I would understand the distinction between religion and spirituality.

In hindsight, I believe several factors coalesced over a period of time to awaken spirituality in me.

The groundwork was prepared by my mother with the parables she had shared with me in childhood. On this foundation, the discourses by Moraribapu and Rameshbhai Oza helped me construct a new belief system less focused on the physical prowess of God and more focused on the deeds. Sadhguru's teachings gave me the courage to explore unconventional avenues without fear. Om Swami's *Kundalini—An Untold Story*, and *The Truth Be Told—A Monk's Memoir*, William Buck's *Ramayana*, and Harold Kushner's *When Bad Things Happen To Good People*, gave me additional courage to explore my relationship with God further and without trepidation.

Understanding spirituality

Sri Eknath's teachings were the icing on the cake. His teachings and writings not only opened up completely new vistas for me, but they also provided me with the tools I would need to explore the spiritual landscape.

At a basic level, I understood God to be the Self and I the self. *Parmatman* and *Atman*. The Self resides in every self, and so God resides in me, in my self too. But beyond that, I believed that I was a standalone, individual entity, as were all other living creatures. We were not connected in any way. That was a fundamental misperception on my part.

If I accepted that the Self resided in the hearts of all living creatures, and that the Self was the reason living beings existed, then it followed that we were all one—that all living creatures were indeed connected through the presence of the Self in their hearts. I now understood what Einstein meant by "the optical delusion of consciousness." One needs to transcend the gross state of consciousness to understand and experience the unity of existence.

With a little difficulty, much pondering, and broad reading, I was able to accept that the Self was nameless and formless. But I also recognized that such a concept would be incomprehensible for most people, as it was for me for more than five decades. Consequently, most require an image to anchor their beliefs and hold their attention while praying.

I now understood the rationale behind why Hinduism gives its followers the liberty of creating their own images of God. In turn, it explained why the Hindu gods were known by so many different names and depicted in thousands of different forms. The images of deities created needed to symbolize power, benevolence, and other godly attributes that were way beyond the realm of a normal human being. Hence, many of the Hindu gods are depicted as many-headed—polycephalic—and with polymelia—with many limbs.

No matter what image an individual conjures up of God, the final path is common to all. Practicing what one believes eventually leads to self-realization. To nirvana. To moksha.

Such a formulation did not make religion and spirituality mutually exclusive. In fact, to my mind, they complement each other.

A religion defines a set of beliefs and practices that a community, as a whole, shares. In this context, I am very comfortable praying. Whereas previously my prayers were full of pleas for pardon and requests for favors, now I humbly ask for forgiveness and offer my gratitude for the Lord's daily blessings and guidance.

Every morning after shower, I sit in the shrine in our home. There, without any variation, I first sing the prayer *Om Jai Jagdish Hare* and follow it by reaffirming the seven resolutions of Kriya Yoga Practice.*

Spirituality gives individuals the freedom to borrow from their religion those beliefs and practices that they believe will help them find

---

* Each resolution is cited, respectively, at the beginning of chapters 1–6 and 9.

peace and harm no one. I believe my spiritual practices have paved the way for me to become a better human being. And not just for myself: but for all in whom the Self resides. For all of us are but one.

I remember experiencing an intense feeling of serenity when this subtle yet significant distinction between religion and spirituality finally dawned on me. I still have the occasional doubt, but I am able to process it with little fear.

Eight:
On Service
to Society

The best way to find yourself is to lose yourself in the service of others.

—Mahatma Gandhi

The practice of meditation helped me clear away a lot of the fog on my spiritual landscape. I started getting answers to the question that had been troubling me for a long, long time: "Who am I?" Detachment from the materialistic world freed me up to seek spiritual growth. It also freed me to think about how I could be of use to society.

"Do give."

One day my father and I were reminiscing about life in Uganda and how limited the opportunities for education were for the local people. By contrast, Shobhi, Arun, and I had completed our professional studies, Nanu was gainfully employed, Mayoor was finishing his undergraduate studies, and little Meeta was doing well in school.

During colonial times the British had created several fine institutions in Uganda including King's College, Budo, and the world-renowned Makerere University. But they afforded quality education to only a small number. The Asian communities had started schools throughout Uganda, and when the time came for higher education, most of them had the resources to send their sons and daughters to the UK, the USA, or India. But for the majority of the local Ugandans, these options for schooling or higher education were not available.

After my father moved to Uganda, he vigorously pursued potential donors in the Asian communities on behalf of poor students because he never forgot how dearly his lack of higher education cost him. His work in the Ministry of Education serendipitously allowed him to learn about how to access government scholarships. This information was never widely circulated. The result was that only a handful of insiders generally benefited from the aid.

I only came to know about this when one of the beneficiaries, Patrick Samambo, came to our home to proudly show the degree certificate he had earned on a scholarship that my father had secured for him. Ever pragmatic, my father told him, "Congratulations. Now get a good job and pay it forward."

I reminded my father of the man I had named Dhanjibhai. This forty-something-year-old gentleman was a homeless Asian in Uganda at a time when there were few others. I suspect he had mental health issues. Several evenings a week, he would stop by our house, expecting us to serve him ice-cold water. He would consume a liter in no time. Unfortunately for us, he would time his arrival while we were in the middle of a game of cricket or badminton. We ignored him until my father commanded us to serve him. The task always fell on me. Reluctantly, I would leave our game, go inside the house and retrieve a bottle of water from the fridge. After he had had his fill, Dhanjibhai would invariably thank me and be on his way. As he turned to leave, I would sprinkle him with the remaining drops. He would take it in stride and laugh.

I thought I got away with my flippant behavior without my father finding out. But decades later, my father revealed he had witnessed me doing it. He shook his head and remarked that it was strange that I had named a destitute, homeless man *Dhanjibhai,* which means a man who owns land, and at the same time I was giving him an unwanted shower. "He only tolerated your behavior because he knew ours was the one home where he could be assured of getting ice-cold water. Do give. But it will mean nothing if you hit them below the belt at the same time."

Founding Polio Children

One bright Sunday morning in December 2002, I was at home in Rochester, reading a newspaper and enjoying the warmth emanating from the fireplace. Through the cinema-sized picture window of our living room, I watched a deer plodding through the foot-thick fresh snow that had fallen during the night. In the background, the pine trees wore beautiful white cloaks. I could not have painted a more heartwarming picture if I had wanted to. It was a Shangri-la moment.

The phone rang. It was Arun, calling from his home in London. He wanted me to join him on a trip to India, where he planned to visit a school for physically disabled children.

A week later, Arun, Mayoor, and I were sitting in the shade of a porch between two office buildings 7,000 miles away in Jodhpur, India.

Arun told us he was reading a local newspaper when a photograph of what appeared to be boys with polio drew his attention. They had come to the UK from India to participate in a tournament for physically disabled children. The newspaper article raved about their success. As a polio survivor, Arun felt motivated to call the boys' coach to offer monetary assistance. The coach suggested, "Why don't you come and visit us first to see how best you can help."

Arun asked me to tag along since I had lived in India for several years and was familiar with the lay of the land. Probably sensing a philanthropic vibe to our trip, my mother encouraged our younger brother Mayoor to join us.

And so there we were, looking at more than 500 children making their way to the dining room. The majority of the children had limbs paralyzed with polio, but there were many others with neurological disorders such as cerebral palsy, and those who had lost one or more limbs to electrocution, snakebites, or vehicular accidents. Some had crutches; a few used tree branches as mobility aids. A lucky few were in wheelchairs pushed along by another disabled child. The rider "paid" the pusher by carrying his or her school bag. But the majority crawled on the pebble-strewn ground. Calluses on their knees and hands bore testament to their struggles.

Mayoor and I had lived all our lives with *a* person with polio. But we had never been anywhere near a group of five, let alone five hundred. What could we possibly do that would make a dent in their suffering? At the time, we felt that even if we had owned a Swiss bank, the help we could provide monetarily would have been inadequate. We were so overwhelmed that for the first day of our visit, we were frozen into inaction.

Rarely had I felt so emotionally drained and so powerless. Memories of the Filipino schoolgirl I sponsored came flooding back. I remembered the smile on her face in the photo the field officer had sent me. *If one child could be helped, then why not 500?* I felt emboldened.

Over the next few days, we came to grips with our emotions. We began interacting with the children individually and in small groups. They started to get used to our presence and their initial reticence to interact with us faded. They shared their challenges, their feelings, their hopes, and their dreams with us. We began to see the souls behind the suffering.

8.1 – Serving children at a school in India supported by Polio Children, 2009

These were children who lived like children. To them, physical limitation was just a nuisance. Elders could worry and fret about it, but they were not going to lose any sleep over it. There were cricket matches to play, *kabaddi* games to compete in, talent shows to prepare for, and a zillion other things to take care of. Life at this institution was far better than life in their villages. There, they were pariahs and strangers to able-bodied children. Here, they were amongst friends—friends who were physically disabled like themselves.

Society saw them as a burden, as extra mouths to feed. Many of them were banished away during weddings and other celebrations, lest they bring ill luck. They were reminded over and over again that they would come to nothing. *Nada.*

"But we are here to prove them wrong," they said with one voice.

The younger kids wanted to know if they would continue to get two curries at lunchtime. So long as there was enough to eat and toys to play with, they were happy to continue to use their classrooms as dormitories at night.

The older boys were anxious about their futures. The schooling at the institution only went as far as high school level. Were they coming to the end of the road? Was higher education just a pipe dream? Or, just as this institution had provided them with a dignified way out of their villages, could it also show them a way into the society that had shunned them not too long ago?

The single most common worry amongst the older girls was whether they would be able to find a marriage partner. No father wanted to bear the "shame" of having an unmarried daughter at home. They were pleasantly surprised to learn that Arun was married—to an able-bodied woman, no less—and had two sons of his own. I am sure his example gave them hope, but they knew the ways of metropolitan London were a far cry from those of rural Rajasthan.

Upon our return home, we started *Polio Children* (now *Polio and Children in Need Charity*), a charity designed to provide nutritional, educational, healthcare, and vocational support to poor children with polio and other neuromuscular disorders.

Fundraising has been a fantastic learning experience for me. In the beginning, if a friend did not donate to the cause, I would take it personally. I felt that he must not trust me or believe in my cause. But as the failures piled up, I accepted that just because I deeply believed in something, I should not expect my friends and acquaintances to do so, too. Nor should I expect them to adopt it with equal passion. People have their own views on benefaction, and I learned to respect them nonjudgmentally. Instead, I decided to continue my efforts with accompanying gratitude for every penny we received and without any preconceived expectations for more. This conscious effort at detachment helped me start noticing the positive happenings.

My daughter Suhina, who was then about five years old, volunteered to help me with stuffing the envelopes when I was mailing out our first newsletter. She did this every year for the next thirteen years until she went to college. When she was in high school, she collected medical and tailoring equipment and delivered them to two programs we supported.

Once at the end of a fundraising event, an elderly lady quietly came up to me and handed me a small bill. She said she wished she could do more to help God's children. Strangers like her and many others who have sent little notes of encouragement and appreciation of our work over the years have been like elixirs.

They motivated us to persevere despite difficult times we faced early on when demands for funding far outstripped our resources. We applied for grants, but they all got turned down. Feeling dejected but undeterred, we continued to appeal to friends and acquaintances through phone calls, setting up booths at conventions, and mailing out newsletters. Lo and behold, we received several mega donations. Since we had witnessed firsthand the consequences of the dual tragedies of physical disability and poverty, there was no question of abandoning ship. We were in for a penny, in for a pound.

We saw children completing high school, graduating from college, getting married, and settling down in gainful employment as teachers, civil servants, doctors, and one even became a Mandarin-speaking tour guide. All that these children needed was hope, for someone to believe in them, and to be treated with dignity. They could do the rest. And they do.

As I reflect on the past eighteen years, the children of these and other non-governmental organizations we have been privileged to serve have taught us more than we have been able to give them through financial aid. They have given us the courage to expand our mission to serve all children in need. I am frequently reminded of my mother's advice from decades earlier:

> **Under the cloak of both wealth and poverty lies God's creation. Respect them for what they are, not for what they have, or have not.**

The experience I gained from operating *Polio Children* gave me the courage to pursue similar ventures on my own.

Aiding recovery

In 2009, I was granted a six-month sabbatical leave from work. My goal was to develop a simple model that would help patients recover from mental illness. The field of behavioral or mental health had made significant strides in the twenty-five years that I had been in psychiatry. In particular, a large number of newer medications had flooded the market. There was tremendous jockeying within pharma to grab the market share. Prozac had been one of the first drugs to enter the scene. Within a few years, dozens more would join the list. The running joke among medical staff at the time was, "Who's bringing lunch today?" as the various pharmaceutical company reps competed for the physicians' lunch hour to feed them and knead them with their newest products.

I was invited and paid handsomely to talk about the new medications to other practitioners in the community. I was under the impression that the invitation was due to my specialized training in psychopharmacology. Once I found out that any psychiatrist willing to give the spiel could do so, I ended my marketing career.

Tons of literature was published to support the remarkable benefits of the new drugs to the patients. As is often the case with science, after an initial period of euphoria over new discoveries, the pendulum starts swinging in the opposite direction. If the new drugs were any better than the old, the improvements were mainly found in their decreased side effects. Their effectiveness on symptoms of the illness was largely comparable. The new drugs were a step forward in the management of mental illness, but they did little to aid the recovery of the patient.

By that, I mean they did little to help patients with chronic mental illness lead a life of their choice in a community of their choice. In mental health, *recovery* means being able to manage the symptoms of the disease, and it is a long process (often lifelong). Whether a person lives with depression, schizophrenia, or alcoholism, during recovery that person needs a safe place to live, to participate in vocational activities, and to develop and maintain social relationships. People with mental illness have hopes and dreams. It is just that they may need specific interventions to help them succeed, just as a person with stroke may need a physical therapist to help him regain strength in his paralyzed limbs, or a speech therapist to help her regain speaking abilities.

To be sure, there have been several reasons for health care providers' failure to move patients' recovery processes along. For most physicians, recovery remains an alien concept. Many erroneously equate *recovery* with *cure*. Few neighborhoods are willing to accommodate group homes for patients with mental illness. And the stigma associated with mental illness is pervasive as ever. Yet I was convinced recovery was possible. But both the focus and locus of care would have to be shifted.

The traditional medical model of care is built around the practices and preferences of the physician. Mental health impacts a patient's mind, his physical well-being, his social relationships, and occupational performance. Therefore, a mental illness, because it has wide-ranging consequences, requires the expertise of more than a psychiatrist. It demands a multidisciplinary approach. The psychiatrist must join forces with psychologists, social workers, nurses, addiction therapists and a host of other practitioners to provide optimal care. Equally important, the focus must shift from the convenience of the healthcare provider to the needs of the patient. This notion gave birth to the term *patient-* or *client-centered care.*

Historically, the locus of care was in a hospital or some similar medical setting. If a patient is expected to live the larger part of his life in the community, then that is where we need to provide rehabilitation services—not in a healthcare setting. Some of the shift had taken place when deinstitutionalization began in the 1960s, when the large back wards—"Big Bins"—in mental institutions were emptied. But we still had a long way to go.

I was cognizant of these challenges and limitations when I set about formulating my version of the recovery model and desktop publishing it in *Recovery-Oriented Mental Health Care: A Guide to Implementing an Evidence-Based Program.*

I recalled the time when I was briefly in private practice. Then, I had witnessed firsthand the effectiveness of talk therapy in the management of common psychiatric disorders such as anxiety and depression. Medications on their own were of limited benefit.

I emphasized the importance of empowering patients and ceding control to them so that they could steer their recovery at their own pace. Support from trusted people is a vital component of recovery. Therefore, in my model, patients would be encouraged to actively engage their family and friends in their recovery. I highlighted that, to the extent possible, patients should be encouraged to pursue recovery from the safety and comfort of their homes while tapping into community resources of their choice.

Lastly, I strongly advocated the addition of a fourth dimension to the traditional three-pronged approach of medication, talk therapy, and social interventions. Some practitioners already considered spirituality as part of social interventions. However, given the critical role of stress in mental illnesses and the subsequent importance of strengthening the mind to cope with stress, I made a case for spirituality as a standalone intervention. I broadened my definition of spirituality to include meditative as well as faith-based practices. To help patients and clinicians appreciate it, I used the analogy of a patient with stroke going to a gym to regain power in his paralyzed limbs. Likewise, a patient with a mental illness needed to go to a mental gym where he could strengthen the "muscles" of his mind.

I named my project "My Goal Recovery" and underlined the importance of giving equal emphasis to all four of the bio-psycho-socio-spiritual interventions in the management of mental illness.

I received a national award for extraordinary achievement in promoting patient-centered care, but in the clinical setting my efforts were met with limited success. Not everyone—whether provider or patient—was willing to adopt this labor-intensive approach. Those who did, however, benefited considerably.

I was immensely pleased when I learnt, soon after I retired, that veterans were being offered formal classes in meditation.

Memorializing Nanu

Since my brother Nanu passed away in 1997, I had wanted to do something to honor his memory. I decided to start a scholarship in his name for students with colostomy. If I could help alleviate some financial pressure for undergraduates who lived with the effects of this medical intervention, they could perhaps enjoy their college life a little more. For the first couple of years, the response rate I received to funding requests was quite good. But then the well dried up. When advertising widely with local gastroenterology medical practices and libraries did not help, I brought down the curtains on the venture.

Perhaps there was a message here. I needed to look beyond the shores of the land of plenty.

Feeding the eagle

In early 2014, I joined Arun on a trip to the country of our birth, Uganda. He was there to participate in a residential course on advanced meditation conducted by Sadhguru's Isha Foundation. My motive was to visit the Queen Elizabeth National Park, famous for its rare but unique tree-climbing lions.

One afternoon when Arun was taking a break from his course, we decided to take a tour of the city and visit the places that had figured so prominently in our childhoods. Both of us had visited the country a few times before, but the trips down memory lane never got stale. Once again, we were attracted to Old Kampala Senior Secondary School. We had many, many pleasant memories of the place, our teachers, our friends, and our sports stars. The latter had brought fame to the school by winning national championships in football and cricket.

As we strolled about the lush green campus, a lady approached us and asked who we were and what we were doing at the school. It's not easy for two Asians to go unnoticed in a school of hundreds of blacks. We told her we were "OB"—Old Boys, a term we had picked up on a previous visit. In a gleeful way that only Africans know how to, she started softly ululating and clapping her hands. Her joy at meeting alumni of her school, albeit senior by decades, was written all over her face. That was the point we reestablished our relationship with our alma mater. Cathy Bisereko would become a most trusted partner.

Over samosas and Cokes, Cathy told us about our school—the good, the bad, and the ugly—in the serene setting of the old library which now served as a meeting room. Arun and I were shocked to learn that the two main challenges the students faced were school fees and textbooks. Both were in utterly short supply. We could not comprehend this state of affairs, as our minds were stuck in the 1970s. When we were students at the school, we never worried about paying fees. As for textbooks, each student was issued a personal copy which was then collected at the end of the school year. Our only concern was how we could land a brand-new copy.

Cathy told us that as the secretary of Old Kampala Alumni Association, she was approached by no less than a dozen parents every year seeking assistance with fees. And these were just the top-ranking students. For the remaining thousand students, the majority struggled with timely payment of school fees.

Cathy shared with us that for any subject, quite often the only textbook available was in the possession of the teacher. The students relied totally on the teacher's notes since the school library, too, was devoid of any textbooks. The new library had been constructed through the generous donation of a benefactor. However, the bookshelves were empty, save for old, moldy journals and government publications, neither of which would help a high school student prepare for his exams.

The next day, we went back to the school and met the star students with their guardians. It was telling that none of the guardians present was a male. Several mothers broke down as they related their personal stories of hardships. Some of them sold rainwater to earn a few pennies. Many could not find work. And then there was Ben Ochieng's story.

Ben was orphaned at a very young age. A good Samaritan of his village, who had seven children of her own, adopted him. A typical day for the thirteen-year-old Ben would begin at dawn when he would rise and herd the goats. He would then help his guardian wrap samosas, which she would sell at the local market later in the day. Still early in the morning, he would walk the six miles to school. His first meal of the day was during the school recess at noon. After school, he walked back home. He would help out with various household chores before dinner. Finally, at 10:00 pm, he would start studying under a paraffin lamp.

Not surprisingly, Ben was thin as a rake when we met him. What he lacked in matter, he more than made up with his sharp mind. He strongly advocated for himself and proudly shared his outstanding grades with us.

Our meeting with the science and maths teachers was equally revealing. Their request was simple: "Provide us with the current editions of the textbooks, and we will ensure that no student is left behind." The teachers had their hearts in the right place. They knew restocking the science labs was an expensive proposition. But if they could get their hands on good textbooks, they could teach their students theory at a depth that would compensate for missing the lab work.

Back in the hotel room, Arun and I were both mulling in our own worlds, but each of us knew what the other was thinking. It was déjà vu *Polio Children*. Time for action.

Before we left Uganda, we visited Queen Elizabeth National Park, stopping to observe where the equator crosses the Kampala–Masaka road. The location is marked by huge white cement circles on both sides of the road. Forty years before, we had zoomed through the midline of the planet as children. On this occasion, however, we savored a beer at a roadside restaurant and absorbed the world passing by.

In the park, we stayed at the Mweya Safari Lodge, where I had the most delicious Nile perch cooked in the traditional way. The following morning, barely twenty minutes' ride away, we saw a pride of lions resting atop several acacia trees.

Once back home, Arun applied to the charities bureau of the UK to register the *Old Kampala Alumni Scholarship Fund*. I would operate the USA branch. We solicited financial support from our friends and invited several to join us. Mayoor, who had spent a year at the school before joining the Asian exodus to the UK in 1972, was as enthusiastic as ever. Arun's schoolmate and friend, Dinesh Dattani, readily agreed. So did mine, Saifuddin Najefy. A few years before, I was quite moved when Saifuddin had called me from his home in London. He was on his way to a pilgrimage in Mecca and wanted me to know that he would be dedicating to my welfare and good health one of the seven *tawaafs*, rounds of circumambulation around the Kaaba, the black cube-shaped structure located at the Grand Mosque in Saudi Arabia. We had the right team.

In our first year of operation, we managed to sponsor the education of twenty-two students. One was Ben. At a subsequent visit to the school, Cathy tearfully related the time she went to Ben's village to let him know that he would be one of our sponsored students. Ben told her that he had been so tired and had lost all direction and hope. The very night she visited him, he had contemplated hanging himself. *Thank you, Lord, for the divine intervention!*

The same year, we delivered the textbooks we had promised. The school authorities put together a ceremony for the occasion. There were songs and dances by the students and speeches by guests from the Ministry of Education. Our football hero, Jimmy Kirunda, who had brought such accolades to our school when we were students there, graced us with his presence. (He would later go on to captain the national team.)

When it was time for us to make our formal presentation, the audio guy played some local music. We clumsily swayed our way to the podium to the great amusement of hundreds of students. Our dancing steps may not have been sharp, but all of us felt an immediate connection with the young folks. The students and teachers were thrilled to meet and hear from our friends Dinesh, Saifuddin, and Aron Desai. They were awed to learn that the student who had topped the school almost fifty years before, Dinesh, was physically amongst them. After the ceremony, we were invited to plant a couple of saplings to commemorate the gift.

Over the years, we have managed to maintain our support of the school despite a rapidly diminishing alumni base. In 2018, we delivered 14,000 books, stocking the school library to the brim.

During one of our early visits to the school, one of the teachers had eloquently put forward her support request: "Please come back to feed the mother eagle that once fed you." We finally did, even if a morsel.

My guru Sri Eknath once said, "The human mind needs meaning in order to live and meaning cannot come from events outside us. It can only come from within."

I feel fortunate that several events in my childhood came together and laid the foundation for nurturing altruistic traits in me. There was that time I witnessed my mother lending money to a friend when she herself had little. And my father's concern for the education of the poor Ugandans and for Dhanjibhai. Meditation gave meaning to these deeds, and engaging in charitable activities made the meaning tangible.

Nine:

On Retirement

I resolve to be mindful of my actions. I will be efficient and try to make the best use of my time and energy.

—from Swami Tyagananda's
Walking the Walk: A Karma Yoga Manual

T hirty-seven years after I came out of medical school, I decided to hang up my white coat—at least my figurative white coat. Long before I started my residency training, psychiatrists had given up the stethoscope, that status symbol many doctors still wrap around their necks. Then, we traded our white coats for the more formal attire of suits and ties. A few of us even changed to bow ties. Scrubs were not for us. They did not jive with our cerebral image—or with the couch.

A few years before I retired, I was mulling about the essential ingredients for a peaceful life. Almost everything I had read about tranquil retirement listed adequate finances as the important element. But I remained unconvinced. So I set about making my own list and came up with a backronym, HAPPY.

H was for *health:*	No amount of money can buy it, so I needed to stay in good shape and make it a top priority.
A was for *assets:*	I should live within my means.
P was for *profession:*	Paid or voluntary, I needed to have a reason to get out of the house every day.
P was for *parivar:*	The Hindi word for *family*—I wanted to enjoy my kith and kin.
Y was for *yoga:*	I wanted to continue to strive for the union of my self with the Self.

HAPPY would become my mantram in retirement.

My financial advisor cautiously agreed with my plan for egression so long as I lived within my means—as if I would blow my savings on a first-class, round-the-world trip! Travel, though, was at the top of my bucket list. Shashi was still working, and retirement was not yet on her horizon. So, I knew that if I wanted to travel, I would have to do so on my own, since I was not keen on joining group tours.

I decided to first test the waters relatively near home in Chile and the Guyanas. Both trips went uneventfully. I made several new friends and returned home unscathed. It was time to take the big plunge.

Pushing my limits on the Annapurna circuit

"Shirish, you follow the porters. We will join you shortly," Surya Thapa Magar, my thirty-year-old guide said, pointing at Bishnu Magar, my porter.

Bishnu was carrying my bright green tote bag on his back with a trump-line across his forehead in the traditional Nepali style. We were off on a two-week trek on the Annapurna Circuit in central Nepal's Himalayan mountain ranges.

I was excited and apprehensive at the same time. I was finally doing what I had planned to do fifteen years before, but because of the Maoist insurgency then, I'd had to cancel. Now, after three months of moderate physical training on the flatlands of upstate New York and equipped with the best attire and gadgets on the market, I was finally setting off. The day before, we had traveled from the nation's capital, Kathmandu, to Chamje in the east. From this starting point, we would be trekking the circuit counterclockwise.

I had gone only a few yards when I saw a group of small children waving at me. I immediately fished bright yellow pencils out from my backpack and beckoned to them. I'd brought the pencils with me specifically for this purpose. The smiles on their faces further brightened an already beautiful morning. The omens were good.

The Himalayan scenery exceeded my wildest expectations. At the base, the ground was covered in lush green foliage crisscrossed with gushing streams. As we began our ascent, now and again we would come across a cut liter soda bottle on a stake firmly planted in the middle of the rushing waters. A hosepipe was attached to the mouth of the bottle. No pumps needed for this ingenuously plumbed water for the nearby village!

When the mountain peaks came into view, the panorama was picture-postcard perfect. My favorite natural wonder is waterfalls. No matter how many I see, big or small, thunderous or trickling, I never tire of them. I have traveled to several countries on itineraries heavily laden with waterfalls. The waterfalls we came across on the Annapurna, though, were a cut above the rest. I stood behind their massive torrents completely surrounded by snow-capped peaks and lush green valleys.

As we made our way up, majestic snow-covered mountains appeared against a dark blue sky, lending their beauty to the 360-degree panorama. For the most part, the trails cut into the mountainside were wide enough for safe trekking. But if transport mules were coming the other way, you had to flatten yourself against the escarpment walls. With each passing day, the vistas became increasingly spectacular until they were sufficient to take one's breath away.

Unfortunately, having one's breath taken away became literally true in my case.

The breathing side of the trek was more challenging to cope with than the muscular exertion. My companion Wolfgang Hartmann, on his fifth trek, was encouraging. "You are doing fine, Shirish. This is no walk in the park, even for us," he would say. Surya kept a subtle but keen eye on me. I tried to apologize for slowing them down, but they waved me off with a chuckle, saying, "This is not a race."

Fueled by *dal-bhat*, the ubiquitous Nepali meal of a soup of spicy lentils served over rice, and refreshed with lemon tea, I struggled on. I always took a head start, so for long stretches of the trek I would be alone with no one else in sight. During these times, I would give myself stern lectures. Part self-motivation speech and part self-upbraiding, I told myself, "Of course you can do it. Are you a quitter? Are you a loser? If it were easy, anyone could do it. Get inside your head and get moving."

I would recite my mantram and pre-determine a set number of steps to take before stopping to catch my breath. Within a couple of days, I managed to go from a mere twenty steps to a full stride of a hundred-plus. Indeed, getting acclimated to the high altitude was helping, but so was repeating the mantram.

On the tenth day of the trek, we arrived at Nar Phedi monastery. When I saw the monastery, located deep down in a valley with a river flowing behind, it set my heart fluttering. Even from a distance, I felt every inch of the monastery oozing with serenity. What would it be like to spend a couple of days meditating here? Not to mention the healing effect the break would have on my tiring physique. Unfortunately, Surya saw through my conniving agenda. So, after a blissful night's rest, we moved on as planned.

On our way to the next stop, we came across a tiny shop in the middle of nowhere run by a beautiful young Nepali woman. Balapuspika was probably in her twenties, and she was dressed in a jogging suit. She had an athletic build and spoke fluent English. Over *chai*, Balapuspika told me she was a university graduate helping her family out while they entertained matrimonial proposals for her. Every day, she walked five miles back and forth from her village carrying supplies. She made it sound like a walk in the park. For a highly educated girl running a rural store, she did not express any resentment or give the slightest hint of self-pity. Her attitude toward life was truly inspirational. She made me appreciate how resolute, adaptable, and family-oriented the Nepali mountain folks were.

We reached Kang La Phedi, *phedi* meaning the "the foot of" in Nepali, late in the morning of day twelve. Kang La Pass, at 17,400 feet, would be the highest point we would traverse the next day.

As there were no teahouses here, the porters put up tents for us. After lunch, I wanted to nap, but Surya insisted we go for a walk in the meadow. We came to a stream where several horses were having a drink after their descent from the pass. Surya went over to talk to the owner, who eyed me, but not Wolfgang, for a few minutes. I did not pay much attention to it and carried on.

At dinnertime, Surya gave us a pep talk on the following day's climb. It was all for my benefit, since Wolfgang had already climbed higher peaks. A couple of times, Surya asked if I had any reservations about making the ascent. I did not know what he was getting at. There were no cable cars to take me up. Turning back was not an option. I wondered if he had doubts about my ability to go over the pass. If so, he should have said so long before. The only way from here was forward.

Around midnight, I was woken up by howling winds. It took me a few minutes to get my bearings as it was pitch black, and the wind flapping against the tent walls made an unbearable din. The thermometer was dropping fast. I covered myself with every article of clothing I could get my hands on and snuggled further into my sleeping bag. As the cold and the noise continued unabated, I started hearing voices and seeing flashing lights. I unzipped the tent door a little but could see nothing. I closed my eyes and started reciting my mantram. In the hope of remaining lucid, I also started reciting meditation passages.

I must have eventually dozed off because the next time I heard a voice, it was Surya's. He had zipped open my tent door and was standing outside with a cup of hot tea for me. The day was just breaking and it was completely still—there was not even the slightest whiff of air.

The ascent was slow going for all of us. Surya stayed no more than a few yards ahead of me, keeping me company. I caught him staring back at me several times. If he was worried about me getting altitude sickness, he could relax. It was my breathing that was killing me! Although I didn't know why at the time, about halfway up, he smiled and took off at his usual pace.

Surya, Wolfgang, Bishnu, and Bhim Dhakal, Wolfgang's porter, all started cheering and waving prayer flags as I summited. They were all laughing and congratulating me. I tried to return the compliment, but they just kept looking at me in what I perceived to be pure admiration.

At the top, Kang La Pass is barely wide enough to accommodate ten people. We took photos in all kinds of poses celebrating the accomplishment. After fifteen minutes, it was time to descend. I looked to Surya to point me to the trail, but he pointed his climbing pole straight down. Before I could protest, he said, "Just follow Bishnu," and turned around.

I stood there thinking, "You've got to be out of your mind."

The downslope, fully covered in scree, appeared to be a ninety-degree drop. I was thinking this had to be one of the team's jokes when Bishnu yelled at me.

He pointed at a spot on the scree in front of me and thumped his foot.

As I gingerly stepped forward, I wondered if it were possible for one to ski down the slope. Moments later, a couple of guys whizzed past me doing just that!

Finally, four hours after I had taken my first tentative step down the pass, and not before I had hit the wall, I stumbled into the teahouse. Once again, there were my companions, waiting for me.

The next evening in Ngwal, over dinner, Surya explained the events of the day before. He was aware that the night in Kang La Phedi would be difficult. He had insisted on the walk in the meadow, hoping it would tire us sufficiently so that we could catch at least a few hours of decent sleep. They, too, had not slept well, having been bothered by rats all night long as they tried to catch a few winks on the kitchen floor.

Surya shared that when he saw me go beyond the midpoint, he was relieved. At that point, he knew he would not have to go back and fetch a horse for me. Then, in his typical understated manner, he said, "I was confident you would make it, so I did not include you in my discussions with the horseman yesterday."

Nice to have someone believe in you, besides yourself.

We celebrated late into the evening. With beer and rum flowing, we gently ribbed each other. Bishnu and Bhim joked that I should stick to conquering illnesses rather than mountain peaks. I complained that if only one of them had kept me company and not sent me ahead by myself, I would have completed the trek without a second breath. They all laughed at my preposterous comment.

With Surya and Bishnu's help and Wolfgang and Bhim's encouragement, over a two-week period I had walked almost 200,000 steps, ascended to 17,000 feet, and survived with only five showers. On top of that, I did not get a single blister!

Without a doubt, the trek was the toughest thing I have ever done in my life, mentally or physically. I often think about the adventure and wonder if I will ever do it again.

9.1 – Conquering Kang La Pass, 2018
Surya, Bhim, Wolfgang, Bishnu, and me

I doubt I will. But if I were to do it, I would train at an altitude much higher than the lowlands of upstate New York. I would also aim to carry fewer pounds on my belly and more on my back. As for companions? Our team would remain unchanged!

An accidental English teacher

My travel plans were proceeding smoothly. I visited family and friends in England, checked off my lifelong desire to visit the Keukenhof Tulip Gardens in Holland, and trekked the Bwindi Impenetrable Forest in Uganda to see mountain gorillas.

During previous tours, my family and I would rush from one site to another, squeezing in everything we could see to get our money's worth.

Now I started taking vacation days during vacations. I would set aside a day here and there to shop the local market, patronize local cafeterias, and visit some local schools. Initially, it felt wasteful and lazy not to be rushing around, but soon I started looking forward to my low-gear activity days.

On one such break day in Bali, I was lolling around in a temple garden when a group of girls approached me. Their dark blue uniforms smartly complemented the bright yellow hijabs draped around their heads. They were out on a field trip. In halting English, they asked if I would answer a few questions to help them complete a project. I said I would be happy to, except that I did not speak Balinese. They started giggling. One took out her cell phone and started reading out questions to me in English. What was my name? Where did I come from? How did I like Bali?

Catching on to their game, I gave short answers, enunciating each word slowly, which a couple of them dutifully wrote down. Ice broken, I asked them to teach me some words in Balinese. About half an hour later, their project complete, they hopped away. Within minutes, I was approached by another group of girls. Word of an English tutor loafing on the temple grounds had spread fast.

9.2 – Teaching English to girls in Indonesia, 2020

In Vietnam, I was followed by a young man for ten minutes before he mustered up enough courage to ask me if I could spare a few minutes and converse with him in English. He had an excellent English vocabulary and wanted to practice speaking it.

I have never figured out why anyone would pick me to brush up on their English. My physical appearance does not advertise English as my mother tongue, nor do I carry around a placard soliciting business. The luck of the draw, maybe? Or perhaps divine guidance propels me along the road of service to others. Whatever the reason, the interactions are thoroughly rewarding.

Escaping winters, tackling mental health

I started spending my winters in India after I retired. Thirty years of shoveling snow in upstate New York was enough.

I had qualified from an Indian university 37 years before, but the healthcare system in the country had changed. I knew that without first getting a feel for the patients and clinicians, I would not be prepared to dive back into clinical practice in India. Plus, my specialty, mental health, was neither well-known nor readily accepted. I thought delivering some guest lectures or running a few workshops would be a nice segue into providing direct patient care. So, I volunteered at a couple of local educational and healthcare institutions.

The first series of talks I gave to master's-level social work students went quite well and came with a few interesting revelations.

Some things hadn't changed. The students all stood when I entered the classroom, just as I used to in school. A student returning from a break well within the allotted time still paused at the open door and asked permission to re-enter.

I am a stickler for time, but the students operated on IST—Indian Stretchable Time, as the common joke went. To enforce timeliness, I stuck a huge notice on the door in bright red letters with commonly recognized symbols: "STOP: Do NOT Enter. Class in Progress." Yet, I repeatedly had latecomers knocking on the door, opening it, and asking permission to enter—completely oblivious to the sign right under their noses! One of the students summed it up nicely when he wrote in the memory book, "You changed our thinking about psychology but not about our watches."

The social work college principal, Dr. Ninad Jhala, and I hit it off quite well. I assisted his faculty in writing a textbook for the undergrads, which Ninad edited. This was a first for the faculty. They were understandably intimidated but performed admirably in the end.

I returned the following year quite enthused. In addition to social work students, I also taught homeopathic interns this time. I was in for a surprise. Immediately after my first talk, a group of interns approached me. They asserted that learning about allopathic medications would not help them in their homeopathic practice as the two branches of medicine prescribe totally different medications. Would it not be more useful, they asked, if I taught them how to deliver psychotherapy? At least this was one aspect of patient management that was common to both our professions.

It was hard to refute their logic. Their enthusiasm to learn something new despite having completed their formal education was also heartening. How could I say no?

A small but dedicated group of 19 interns came together and formed the inaugural Cognitive Behavior Therapy class. They came to be known as CBT wallahs. Over the next six weeks, we plodded along, using Western developed protocols to alter Eastern ways of thinking and behaving. It was one of the best teaching experiences I ever had.

I was retired and had shed my professorial airs. I encouraged everybody to participate in the discussions. There would be no such thing as a dumb question or a dumb answer. We abandoned the traditional classroom setup in favor of a circle of chairs. The interns were not used to my kind of teaching or being treated as yaars, friends. I tried to keep the momentum going by bringing snacks for the breaks. I would join them for sweet masala chai at the roadside kiosk, and we had meals together a few times. The scene was set to achieve our mutual goal of improving patient care.

As the students and interns began feeling comfortable with me, several approached me individually to seek my professional advice for their personal problems. I understood that they felt safe to talk about these issues on their home ground. I was also aware of the paucity of psychiatric providers in the area and the strong stigma still attached to mental illness.

9. 3 – CBT Wallahs, 2019

Assuming their issues would be medication related, I agreed to meet with them. But none were. They all pertained to relationship issues. The most shocking part to me was the cavalier manner in which several of them expressed suicidality.

Bharti was a tall slim girl. Her almond-shaped eyes glistened behind oversized glasses. She had long, lustrous black hair tied in a bun atop her head and was dressed in blue *shalwar kameez*.

She was having difficulty sleeping and wanted to know if I could recommend any medication. As we explored the causes of her insomnia, she revealed she had been dating a young man in her class for the past three years. With the completion of their internships approaching, they wanted to get married. However, her parents were opposed to the marriage because the boyfriend came from a different caste. She came from a well-to-do family and both her parents were educated. They warned her that she would jeopardize her younger sister's marriage if she decided to marry out of caste. She had expected her parents would object. She was not clinically depressed. Just confused.

For the next half hour, we explored her options. She agreed to get the elders of her community to talk to her parents. She also thought if her boyfriend's parents would speak with hers, it may work. She tossed around a few other ideas.

I asked her what she would do if all attempts failed.

"I will commit suicide," she said, shrugging her shoulders.

I thought I had misheard her given the nonchalant way she responded and because of my hearing impairment. But she repeated the statement and again showed no emotion.

Over the next three months, I came across similar statements from several other students. The circumstances were different—relationship issues, social disgrace, finances, failure. But the ultimate resolution in their minds, if nothing else worked, was the same.

Suicide.

The primary causes of suicide in India were very different from what I had seen in patients with mental illnesses in the West. In the West, most took their own lives because of depression or alcohol or substance abuse. Social issues were a contributing factor in some cases but were rarely the primary reason. In India, I was learning that it was often the opposite. It made me think about my own mother's suicide attempt in my childhood. As if I needed any further validation, about the same time, a twenty-year-old distant nephew of mine took his own life after a breakup with his girlfriend.

I felt an urgent desire to do something. A message needed to go out that spoke to the value of life, that minimized the stigma associated with mental illness, and that let people know help was available—a message that *someone* cared for them, a message that gave hope to people who felt they were at the end of their tether.

I rallied the CBT wallah interns and solicited volunteers from the social work students. Our goal was to start small and on the home pitches. We would create posters and post them on college campuses and in local clinics. The volunteers would be the first points of contact and would triage callers according to their needs. Even though they were few in number, we would solicit the support of local psychiatrists and other mental health care providers.

Our initiative raised awareness amongst the participants and their colleagues. They embraced the idea wholeheartedly and recognized the urgency with which it needed to be addressed. They accepted that if even one life were saved, the effort would be worth it.

However, the bu reaucratic maze we encountered proved to be much harder to negotiate than we anticipated. So, at the time of this writing, the venture remains a work in progress.

Ten:
Epilogue—
Raindrops

Of all that is wonderful in the human being, our most glorious asset is the capacity to change ourselves.

—Eknath Easwaran, *Conquest of Mind*

A s I look back and ponder the sources of the lessons I have learnt, an image of raindrops falling on a vast landscape comes to mind. I see seedlings in various stages of germination spread across an otherwise mostly barren land. The first leaves of the seedlings are wide open, like the palms of a man's hands. They face the sky as if thanking it for the life-sustaining nourishment it has sent.

My academic mind once yearned for spiritual knowledge nicely packaged into one volume like the medical textbooks I had read all my life. When I found none, I turned to Hindu scriptures. I hit the jackpot with Sri Eknath Easwaran's *The Essence of the Upanishads*. And just like the Upanishads, I discovered that pearls of wisdom come from many sources: scriptures, sages, even common men and women—men like the soft-drink seller in Zambia and women like my mother.

I have by no means fully incorporated the wisdom I've encountered from spiritual and other disciplines. I am far from a saint. My progress in places is uneven. I grew up in a relatively strict vegetarian family. Eggs were an occasional transgression. After leaving home, I followed a full-fledged non-vegetarian diet for a couple of decades before finally settling down to a pescatarian diet. My dietary preference conflicts with my spiritual motives, yet I have come to accept it. British fish and chips remains my favorite meal and a draught beer in a pub, my favorite bevvy.

As I've internalized my thoughts and experiences over the years, I have begun to understand myself. Recognizing and acknowledging my fiery temper was demoralizing and depressing. But when I accepted it, I felt liberated. This first step towards viewing myself from other people's eyes and then trying to understand my corresponding thoughts and behaviors paved the way for further self-analysis. In the process, I experienced emotional turmoil, which was quite severe at times, but my meditative practices helped ameliorate much of it.

Eventually, I formed a mental image of my emotions. They took the form of a wave moving through a cylindrical tube. Events that made me happy manifested as peaks, and those that made me sad as valleys.

Before I started to meditate regularly, my tube's height was as big the Brooklyn-Battery Tunnel. The huge highs the tunnel allowed were very pleasant experiences, but the deep lows were equally melancholic. If I could reduce the diameter of the tube, the feelings associated with positive experiences would be reduced in intensity, but so would those attached to the negative ones. I set the goal of constricting the Brooklyn-Battery Tunnel into a thin cable. In this, I found Swami Tygananda's explanation of the concept of attachment-detachment most useful.

In a nutshell, the Swami describes how desire *(kama)* is linked to action *(karma)*, which can bring about sorrow *(duhkha)*. Detachment breaks this link and ends sorrow. There are several ways to affect detachment. The one that most appeals to me is *karma yoga*, "...studying, analysing, and controlling our engagement with the world through *work* [my emphasis]."

I can't say my emotional roller-coaster is housed in a thin wire all the time. But the analogy has worked well for me. Whenever I anticipate that a situation will be out of the ordinary, I visualize a current with small peaks and shallow valleys flowing through a thin wire. The image helps me to apply the brakes on any untoward thought or behavior the situation may engender.

At other times, when I find myself getting tensed up in relation to a thought or in anticipation of an event, I visualize myself turning a crankshaft as if I were unwinding a cable. Invariably, I start feeling relaxed as if the tautness in my body had been slackened.

These cognitive approaches have helped me in many different ways.

I have moderate to severe hearing impairment, even with hearing aids in both ears. Those who have this disability will appreciate how irritating it is to ask others to repeat what they have said. It is even more so when you misinterpret what someone has said and give a tangential response. I have come to accept, and sometimes even join in, the laughter my flub-ups generate. But I avoid groups and have become a bit of a recluse. The coronavirus disease (COVID-19) pandemic, while it lasts, has provided an additional valid reason for me to continue to isolate myself.

With better control of my emotions, I have become more patient. I have learnt to ignore many of my pet peeves. My obsession with timeliness persists, but I no longer chastise students for tardiness.

At home, I am better at handling disagreements with my wife and my daughter. Between learning to let go and minimizing drama in my responses, I have found that most contentious issues simply dwindle away. I frequently remind myself of the sage's advice: "Give and forgive."

By shifting focus from myself to others, I have freed up space in my head and my heart for spiritual growth.

The sage Rameshbhai Oza often used to say, "Jeev mahan no bhukyo che," meaning, "The human mind starves for respect." I now find it easy to show respect to people no matter their standing in society, their material wealth or lack thereof, or their academic credentials. The effect on both sides has been magical. In giving, I am receiving.

10.1 – My daughter, Suhina, me, and my wife, Shashi, 2014

While I paid close attention to my daughter's cerebral and spiritual growth, Shashi ensured that she freely pursued her childhood passions. From a very young age, Suhina loved to dance. She would insist that I videotape her as she danced to her choreography of the Bollywood music. When she was about 7 years old, Shashi introduced her to classical Indian dances. Avoiding many of the distractions that come across a schoolgirl's life, Suhina successfully managed keep up her dance practice for the next nine years. Following the completion of formal training, she made her debut on stage, called *Arangetram*. Her solo performance lasted for three hours and was attended by a couple hundred guests. It was one of the proudest moments of our lives.

I am pleasantly surprised by the number of her friends and younger cousins who solicit her advice and seek her support during difficult times. I have seen her become more empathetic and a patient listener over time.

As a parent, my hope is that my daughter will not develop any of my insecurities. From the time when she was very young, I kept a watchful eye on her likes and dislikes, her strengths and weaknesses. I wanted to help her strengthen her positive traits and minimize, if not eliminate, her negative traits. I became aware that to do so, I would have to lead by example. With the guidance of my compassionate mother, the teachings of an enlightened guru, and my reading and meditating on gnostic scriptures, I hope, to paraphrase Gandhi, that I have been and will continue to become the change that I see in my daughter and in her future.

I am an ordinary person who used ordinary methods that led to extraordinary life-changing experiences. I discovered that meditation was the supreme component of spirituality. I believe the raindrops of lessons I've had in my life have fallen on fertile ground, and I hope my story inspires others to take up meditation, and in the process, find their selves in the Self.

Om mani padme hum.

Enlightening Literature

Buck, William. *Ramayana: King Rama's Way—Valmiki's Ramayana told in English Prose*. Los Angeles: University of California Press, 1976.

Easwaran, Eknath. *The Bhagavad Gita for Daily Living, Vol. 1: The End of Sorrow*. Tomales, CA: Nilgiri Press, 1975.

Easwaran, Eknath. *The Bhagavad Gita for Daily Living, Vol. 2: Like a Thousand Suns*. Tomales, CA: Nilgiri Press 1979.

Easwaran, Eknath. *The Bhagavad Gita for Daily Living, Vol 3: To Love is to Know Me*. Tomales, CA: Nilgiri Press, 1988.

Easwarn, Eknath. *Conquest of Mind: Take Charge of Your Thoughts and Rehshape Your Life Through Meditation (3rd ed)*. Tomales, CA: Nilgiri Press, 2010.

Easwaran, Eknath. *The Dhammapada: A Classic of Indian Spirituality*. Tomales, CA: Nilgiri Press, 2007.

Easwaran, Eknath. *Essence of the Upanishads: A Key to Indian Spirituality*. Tomales, CA: Nilgiri Press, 2009.

Easwaran, Eknath. *The Mantram Book: A Practical Guide to Choosing Your Mantram & Calming Your Mind*. Tomales, CA: Nilgiri Press, 2008.

Easwaran, Eknath. *Passage Meditation: Bringing the Deep Wisdom of the Heart into Daily Life*. Tomales, CA: Nilgiri Press, 2008.

Easwaran, Eknath. *Timeless Wisdom: Passages for Meditation from the World's Saints & Sages*. Tomales, CA: Nilgiri Press, 2008.

Easwaran, Eknath. *Words to Live By: Short Readings of Daily Wisdom*. Tomales, CA: Nilgiri Press, 2005.

Hart, William. *Vipassana Meditation: As Taught by S.N. Goenka*. San Francisco: HarperOne, 1987.

Kushner, Harold S. *When Bad Things Happen to Good People*. New York: Anchor Books, 2004.

Om Swami. *If Truth Be Told: A Monk's Memoir*. India: Harper Element, 2015.

Om Swami. *Kundalini—An Untold Story: A Himalayan Mystic's Insight into the Power of Kundalini and Chakra Sadhana*. India: Jaico Publishing House, 2016.

Sadhguru (Vasudev, Jaggi). *Mystic's Musings*. Reading, UK: Wisdom Tree, 2004.

Simone, Cheryl and Sadhguru Jaggi Vasudev. *Midnights with the Mystic: A Little Guide to Freedom and Bliss*. Charlottesville, VA: Hampton Roads, 2008.

Swami Tyagananda. *Walking the Walk: A Karma Yoga Manual*. Chennai, Tamil Nadu: Adhyaksha, 2013.

List of Photographs

1.1 – My mother and father, c. 1949

1.2 – The Patel siblings, 1994

2.1 – Nitin and me, 1984

6.1 – Sri Eknath Easwaran. Photo available on the Blue Mountain Center of Meditation website, http://yameditation.org/blog/2013/9/17/eknath-easwaran-life-is-a-trust.

8.1 – Serving children at a school in India supported by Polio Children, 2009

9.1 – Conquering Kang La Pass, 2018

9.2 – Teaching English to girls in Indonesia, 2020

9.3 – CBT wallahs, 2019

10.1 – My daughter, Suhina, me, and my wife, Shashi, 2014

My Thanks

Ms. Rachel Hall: An editor par excellence. Thank you for your encouragement and for humoring my obsessive traits. Sharing your personal experiences at appropriate places helped validate that I was not too much off the mark! If writing was revealing, going through the editing process and seeing the final product emerge was rewarding.

Mr. Ramesh Nadoda of Sanskruti Digital: Thank you for rescuing and restoring my parents' old photograph.

Miblart: Thank you for your patience and creativity in designing the book cover.

Mr. Ken Waisanjo of Great IT Servicest: Thank you for your IT support.

My Commitment

Proceeds from the sales of this book will be donated to:

Polio and Children In Need Charity
PolioChildren.org

Committed to making children with polio and other neuromuscular disorders and those coming from economically disadvantaged backgrounds independent and productive citizens of society through educational, nutritional, healthcare, and vocational support.

&

Helping Underprivileged Students Of
Old Kampala Senior Secondary School
Achieve Their Dreams

Old Kampala Alumni Scholarship Fund
OKASFund.org

Dedicated to helping academically gifted but economically disadvantaged students of Old Kampala Senior Secondary School, Kampala, Uganda, achieve their dreams.

CPSIA information can be obtained
at www.ICGtesting.com
Printed in the USA
LVHW011115070121
675555LV00006B/872